DEFAMATION FACTORY

Kaiter Enless

DEFAMATION FACTORY

The Sordid History of the ADL

Preface by Tomislav Sunić

Reconquista Press

© Reconquista Press, 2018
www.reconquistapress.com

ISBN 978-1-912853-03-8

CONTENTS

Preface by Tomislav Sunić 11

Introduction 17

   I   The Founding Lie: The Leo Frank Case (1913-1915) 19

   II   The ADL vs. Henry Ford (1915-1933) 31

   III   WWII & the ADL Mafia (1933-1985) 53

   IV   Pollard's Gambit (1984-1990s) 73

   V   The ADL vs. Lyndon LaRouche 79

   VI   Bullock's Blunder & LaRouche's Return 85

   VII   "Hate" Goes Viral: The ADL in the Digital Age (1990s-present) 97

Sources 151

"[T]he Anti-Defamation League for many years has maintained a very important, confidential investigative coverage of Arab activities and propaganda. (…) Our information, in addition to being essential for our own operations, has been of great value and service to both the United States State Department and the Israeli government. All data have been made available to both countries with full knowledge to each that we were the source."

Letter from Benjamin R. Epstein, National Director, Anti-Defamation League to Saul Joftes, Executive Secretary, B'nai B'rith, July 7, 1961.

★

"They're Liars. They're THE Defamation League."
Ezra Levant on the ADL, 2017

★

"It's understandable that many casual Internet browsers readily accept as valid spurious quotes attributed to me. What's less excusable is the readiness of some professional journalists to uncritically accept them, merely on the say-so of an organization, such as the ADL or SPLC, which has an easily verifiable record of distortion and partisan bias."

Mark Weber, February 2, 2018 (IHR)

PREFACE

There is such a huge literature on Jews that it makes one wonder whether it is necessary at all to add more books on this subject. For the most part, the literature on Jews, at least as far as our postmodern discourse is concerned, depicts them as eternal victims of irrational prejudice by non-Jews. Hence, Jewish victimhood — either real or surreal — must now be projected worldwide as an educational tool for preordaining Jews as moral pillars of the whole of humanity, who, in addition, must be appointed to serve as the conscience of always aggressive and unpredictable Gentiles. Even the literature critical or hostile to Jews, which carries as a rule the label, "anti-Semitic," plays an important role in bolstering Jewish identity. Were there no more anti-Semites around, it is questionable how much longer Jewish identity in its actual shape would survive. Likewise, if all present anti-Semites were to disappear for good, a new brand of anti-Semitism would likely need to be invented.

In the following chapters, while focusing on the powerful Jewish agency the Anti-Defamation League (ADL) Kaiter Enless explains a specific Jewish binary behavior transpiring in constant fear of sudden anti-Jewish outbursts, on the one hand,

and on the other, in the obsessive Jewish quest for the real or purported "anti-Semite." The merit of this book is that its author delves into semantic distortions used in the ADL discourse on potential or purported critics of Jews. While it is today acceptable to talk in general about "German crime" or "Russian crime" or "American crime," without criminalizing the entire German, Russian or American nation, the same generic usage of the word "Jew," let alone the verbal construct "Jewish crime," is unacceptable and even, as is the case in modern Europe today, subject to *criminal sanctions*. The substantive "Jew," even when used in a neutral political context, must be avoided. It should not come as a surprise that even the short, high-pitched English phoneme "Jew" /dʒuː/ is getting more and more replaced by a somewhat attenuated low-pitched adjective consisting of the two English syllables "Jewish," thought to be able to offer some safe haven to a writer venturing into critical comments on some aspects of Jewish behavior, albeit always on guard not to cross the line, lest they get branded an "anti-Semite."

Similar recourse to the adjectivization of the noun "Jew" is taking place in French and German speaking media and scholarship. Mentioning solely and out of appropriate context, the German barrel sounding and prolonged two-syllable noun "Jude" ("yoo-deh"), or a shrill French one syllable noun "juif" /ʒɥif/ in the German or French languages respectively, even if no Jew-bashing is intended, sounds disturbing in the ears of Jews.

PREFACE

Keeping this in mind, it comes as no surprise that ever since its foundation the ADL has maintained a keen interest in having the last word in shaping public discourse—first in America, later in Europe. Having realized the power of words, the early founding fathers of the Anti-Defamation League decided to adorn themselves with this nice, abstract, flowery, and lachrymose title providing an impartialness signified in the public eye, rather than adding a preceding and earsplitting qualifier "Jew" or "Jewish." The hypothetical, albeit more appropriate denomination i.e., "the Jewish Anti-Defamation League," would barely have the same resonance of impartiality amidst American citizens today.

Enless' book offers a handy overview of ADL activities over the last century in America. This semi-secretive organization has managed, under cover of a humanitarian jargon and tolerance preaching, to cover up its own, often murky and criminal affairs. For readers who grew up in the former communist universe, the awesome similarities between the former communist newspeak in Eastern Europe and the present ADL newspeak in America cannot be overlooked.

Enless' book reads like a police report on a suspect pronounced guilty, yet who never ever considers entering a guilty plea. Instead, the suspect deftly reroutes criminal charges against him by declaring *himself* a victim of hate. Thus, the murder of a young Gentile girl by a Jew in Atlanta, Georgia in

1913, and his subsequent lynching by an angry Gentile mob came as an excellent legal framework for legitimizing the future activities of the ADL.

Today, we take for granted the usage of the expression "hate speech," as if this expression had been embedded in English and American literary and juridical baggage ever since the birth of the English language or the birth of Geoffrey Chaucer. It is often forgotten that this equally abstract, generic expression is of recent provenance, practically unknown in the modern English language until the end of the 70s of the 20th century. Nowadays, this newspeak expression "hate speech" is being heftily championed by the ADL and similar institutions promoting peace and racial tolerance. The expression "fighting against hate" has become a major battle cry of the ADL, also entering into the daily parlance of modern citizens and their politicians who seldom bother to examine the origin of this expression, the motives of its inventors, and the purpose of its usage. The author notes that, "a world without hate… is, after all, a phrase which the ADL liked so much that they had it trademarked."

The book also sheds light on verbal inversion carried out by the ADL and its Gentile minions and how their linguistic manipulations result in the inversion of political reality. Or to put it more academically, verbal inversion always leads to the reversal of a thesis. This is particularly true in the modern Western judiciary and scholarship which are

PREFACE

becoming more and more inclined to arbitrary decision-making, always ready to clamp down on free speech advocates by declaring every non-conformist thought offensive or criminal. For instance, Henry Ford, a famous American car maker, who is also mentioned in the book, was himself, along with thousands of unnamed American activists, the subject of such thesis reversal. The ADL had initiated a smear campaign against Ford after Ford himself had first drawn attention to legal improprieties of the ADL.

The last chapter of the book leaves the reader holding his breath. The new viral world of the Internet is now providing the ADL with awesome tools for silencing intellectual dissent. However, it also opens up new avenues of dissent for free speech advocates and activists.

Tomislav Sunić, PhD
Zagreb, September, 2018

INTRODUCTION

Why do we talk of politics? Why do we engage in that stressful, brain-wracking contest of ever-warring tribes when we can just ignore the whole damnable mess? I cannot, nor shall I attempt to, speak for anyone but myself, and so I shall tell you why I speak about politics. I speak about politics because, on matters of first principal, chaos, entropy, is the enemy of civilization whilst all that moves to order and truth – all that holds chaos at bay – is its soothing balm.

As an American I care deeply about my country, and our traditions, foremost among which is freedom of speech. Without the ability to speak as one see's fit (without violating law) all other freedoms become impossible. As such, the maintenance of this tradition is of considerable practical importance.

Therefore, when one discovers a powerful entity which directly threatens this societal cornerstone, it would be, not just irresponsible, but downright unconscionable to ignore the profligate, so-called "hate watch" group known as the Anti-Defamation League of B'nai B'rith (ADL). However, I shall show you, incontrovertibly, that the ADL is anything but. Indeed, I shall show you that they are the precise opposite of a group looking out for the common good, for the man defamed, I shall show you that the ADL is, in no uncertain terms, an often hateful, slanderous and law-breaking guild of ethno-tribalist radicals who stand for everything they decry. It is the very summit of irony that the organization which brands itself as the premier outfit for fighting against defamation is one of the primary, generative machines thereof.

Chapter I

THE FOUNDING LIE: THE LEO FRANK CASE (1913-1915)

Despite the fact that the ADL ostensibly operates under the auspices of being keen to "stop the defamation of the Jewish people," the events which lead to the founding of the group had absolutely nothing to do with defamation and absolutely everything to do with a savage, cold-blooded murder. The murder of an innocent, 13-year-old girl.

On Saturday, April 26, 1913, little Mary Phagan, a young girl who toiled for the well known National Pencil Company of Atlanta, Georgia, stopped by her place of work to obtain $1.20 in earnings from the company superintendent, Leo M. Frank. She would never be seen alive again.

Her body was later found in the Pencil Company basement, mutilated. Her undergarments were torn and ugly bruises stood out upon her neck and the whole of her body was covered in the ashes of the nearby incinerator. She had been strangled to death with a wrapping cord, likely after the assailant failed to rape her.

It was Confederate Memorial Day.

The murder set the town awhirl with the denizens of the town demanding justice. After a thorough investigation many were suspected but none more so than the lecherous superintendent, Leo Max Frank. Frank's guilty verdict was announced on August 25th, 1913. Frank was eventually convicted of the grisly, barbaric crime and sentenced to death by hanging. On October 1913, after Frank's conviction, Adolf Kraus, then president of the Jewish-American fraternal order, B'nai B'rith, in conjunction with Sigmund Livingston, a prominent Jewish attorney, created the Anti-Defamation League of B'nai B'rith which issued forth this statement of purpose in their League charter:

> "The immediate object of the League is to stop, by appeals to reason and conscience and, if necessary, by appeals to law, the defamation of the Jewish people. Its ultimate purpose is to secure justice and fair treatment to all citizens alike and to put an end forever to unjust and unfair discrimination against and ridicule of any sect or body of citizens."

Despite the best efforts of Livingston and Kraus' newly formed Anti-Defamation League as well as the masonic inspired B'nai B'rith, Frank was eventually executed, but not through lawful jurisprudence. Rather, he was let off the hook by an outgoing governor, John M. Slaton, after a great deal of back-door dealing. Frank's sentence was transmogrified from death by hanging to life behind bars. The denizens of the town were so enraged by this obvious corruption of justice that they decided to take the law into their own hands and subsequently dragged Frank from the courthouse and summarily executed him. He was lynched from an oak tree in Mary Phagan's hometown of Marietta, Georgia on August 16, 1915. The Phagan Family's house was the last thing Leo Frank ever saw.

Contrary to the widely held misconception that Frank was the first Jew ever to be lynched, he was far from it. In 1868, a Jewish store owner in Franklin, Tennessee named S.A. Brierfield and a black worker, Lawrence Bowman were lynched by initiates of the KKK for supporting The Reconstruction; in 1915, the Jewish writer and convicted murderer, Albert Bettelheim was lynched only two days before Frank himself was slain. What markedly differentiated the Frank Case from the previously mentioned incidents was the enormous media firestorm that ensued and the way in which the case transformed the sociopolitical landscape of the region.

In the many years since the Phagan murder, Leo Frank has become a venerated figure among many Jewish-Americans; so much so that it might be said without hyperbole, that he is viewed by the ADL as their patron saint; as a man whose death serves as a reminder of the depths of depravity to which man can sink when in the grip of xenophobic hatred. This holy martyr reverence shines through in many of the articles written by members of the League that are still archived on the site to this day. To provide some context to the ADL's feeling about the Frank Case consider this excerpt from their article, *Remembering Leo Frank*,

> "During this same time, an event in Georgia made the need for the organization painfully clear. Leo Frank, a Jewish businessman who moved to Atlanta to manage his family's pencil factory, was convicted of the rape and murder of a 13-year-old female employee, following a trial that was defined by anti-Semitism."

Note the last line, "*following a trial that was defined by anti-Semitism.*" This idea is one oft touted by modern historians (especially liberal ones). Given the prevalence of the notion that Frank was innocent of the crime but was hanged due to rampant anti-Semitism, Southern idiocy and the tendency to always defer to perceived authorities, (a tendency which runs counter to many of the claims of American egalitarians – but more on that later) most of the American public tends to believe the blood-libel narrative as well. But is it actually true? Was Frank actually innocent of killing Mary Phagan?

Short answer, no. He was most decidedly guilty. With that said, let us turn our attention to the facts indicating just that.

THE FOUNDING LIE

Pertinent Facts Concerning Leo Frank's Guilt:

Fact 1 – P.A. Flak, a fingerprint expert who was tasked with investigating the Phagan murder crime scene, lifted fingerprints belonging to two men, Newt Lee, the Afro-American night-watchman of the National Pencil Company who had first discovered Phagan's body and Leo Frank.

Fact 2 – Lee testified in court that Frank had called him at night, previous to the discovery of the corpse, to ask if everything was alright. This, Newt Lee stated, was exceedingly strange, as Frank had never before directly telephoned him.

Fact 3 – Frank explicitly stated whilst testifying at his trial that he did not know Mary Phagan by name yet numerous female employees of the Pencil Factory testified to the fact that they had seen Frank talking with Phagan on various occasions, sometimes putting his arm upon her shoulder. One young woman, a 16-year-old named Dewey Hall stated in court that Frank would talk to Mary Phagan "two or three times a day." These same women also testified to the fact that Frank was possessed of a decidedly lascivious nature and would regularly make sexual advances upon female factory workers, sometimes slipping away with them into a private room for suspiciously long stretches of time.

Fact 4 – Leo Frank told the police that John Gantt, a factory worker who was a friend of Mary Phagan's, had been "intimate" with the dead girl. This obviously contradicts Frank's earlier statement that he did not know Phagan at all. For, after all, how could Frank have known Gantt had any ties to Phagan if Frank did not even know Phagan by name? Clearly, Frank was lying.

Fact 5 – Initially the two primary suspects were Leo Frank and an employee, Jim Conley, and it is believed by many today who think Frank innocent that Jim Conley was the real killer. However, Conley worked on the ground floor for his entire shift, this means that if he had been the killer he would have had to attack Mary Phagan almost as soon as she entered the building where there was effectively zero privacy given the constant stream of people. Conley was not perceived as being particularly intelligent, this coupled with the fact that there was nowhere to kill and effectively hide someone at his work station undetected put him entirely out of the realms of possibility as a suspect. Furthermore, Leo Frank, however, did have a secured area upon the second floor where one could do all manner of things without sight or sound from anyone; Frank also admitted to the fact that he had been alone with Mary Phagan upon the second floor where he (quite a tall man) could have easily killed her without oversight.

Fact 6 – Newt Lee, the night watchman who was an early primary suspect in the case and who had no motives against anyone involved, arrived at the Pencil Factory before Phagan's body was discovered and found Frank there and told him he would sleep in the basement (where Lee ultimately discovered Phagan's body). Frank refused to let him and further forced him to leave, saying that Lee had to

"Have a good time." This was not only extremely odd, it was also against the National Pencil Company's corporate policy which stated that the night watchman, once he entered the building, was not to leave until he had passed along his keys to the day watchman. What this suggests is that Frank knew Phagan's body was in the basement and that, if Lee retreated to the factories bowels, the crime would be discovered.

Fact 7 – Lee left as Frank commanded but returned later at six to discover Frank so nervous and agitated that he could not do even the most basic of functions, such as operating his time clock. However, it should be noted that two mechanics who worked at the factory disputed Lee's story, with both claiming that Frank had acted perfectly normally.

Fact 8 – On April 30th 1913, a friend of Mary Phagan's, a 15-year-old named George Epps, testified that Phagan was afraid of Leo Frank because he had flirted with the little girl and made several sexual advances towards her.

Fact 9 – May 9th, 1913, a young girl who worked at the factory named Monteen Stover stated that she had arrived to work at the National Pencil Factory at 12:05 PM the day of the murder (near the same time Phagan arrived) and that when she arrived Frank was not in his office. This directly contradicts Franks testimony in which he stated he had stayed in his office the entire time the murder was supposed to be taking place at the factory.

Fact 10 – June 3rd, 1913, Minola McKnight, Leo Frank's Afro-American cook, states in a statement to local police authorities that Frank was exceedingly nervous, agitated and also remarked that he drank heavily after he had returned home the night Mary Phagan was murdered.

Fact 11 – Jim Conley, though initially one of the prime suspects due to his own admissions of aiding in the murder and history of violence (he once threatened his wife and an employee at gunpoint), was a known serial liar and his story continuously changed throughout the course of the case and often made no sense at all.

Fact 12 – July 30th, 1913, Frank had testified that he had not seen Mary Phagan's body at the undertaker's yet a man named W.W. (Boots) Rogers, testified that Frank had indeed been to the undertaker's and had there seen the body of the young, murdered girl.

Fact 13 – Jim Conley testified that he had often acted as a look-out man for Frank during his liaisons with young factory works. Conley also testified to the fact that he had helped Frank move Phagan's body after the murder (letters found near Phagan's body were noted to be in Conley's handwriting) and that Frank had confessed to the killing and was so shaken with what he had done that he had gripped Conley for support. Though many points in Conley's story changed markedly from its first telling, these points always remained consistent. On August 7th a railroad worker named C.B. Dalton testified to the fact that he had often met with women in the National Pencil Factory's basement and that, during these libidinous ventures, Conley had often acted as the lookout – a fact which only reinforces the veracity of Conley's testimony. Furthermore, Dalton went on to state that, on numerous occasions during his ventures to the factory, he had seen Frank privately meeting with women. Also, two hundred dollars were known to have been on the premises of the Pencil company, this was the same amount of money which Jim Conley said Frank had showed to him during their meeting after the murder.

Lastly, let us examine this notion set forth by the Frank defense team and carried on by the ADL that the whole arc of the case was carried, in whole or in part, by racial bigotry and lay it swiftly to rest. Contrary to popular belief, the South, at the time, was not anti-Semitic but rather philo-Semitic. The racial animus during the trial was not, principally, directed towards Frank, but rather, towards Jim Conley, a negro janitor who worked for the National Pencil Company. Conley was, admittedly, a drunkard and a liar, a man of low-repute, but the vitriol he received passes all boundaries of decency. For instance, during the course of the trial, Conley was targeted by numerous instances of abuse from Frank's defense attorneys, Luther Rosser, Rueben R. Arnold and Frank Hooper.

Arnold insisted that Conley was a "a drunken, crazed negro, hard up for money."

Hooper contended that the black janitor was a "Dr. Jekyll" who, "when the shades of night come, throws aside his mask of respectability and is transformed into a Mr. Hyde."

Rosser scathingly remarked that Conley was "a filthy, lying nigger" who probably snorted "tons of cocaine."

However, the presiding Prosecutor, Hugh Dorsey (whose sister was married to the son of Luther Rosser), took umbrage to the remarks of the defense and also wholly denied that Frank was being tried due to some untoward feelings concerning the Jewish People upon whom he remarked, "This great people [the Jews] rise to heights sublime, but sink to the depths of degradation, too, and they are amenable to the same laws as you or I and the black race."

The outspoken agrarian populist and publisher, Tom Watson, wrote extensively and critically of the case, paying special attention to the charges of anti-Semitism; his publication, *Watson's Magazine*, echoed sentiments similar to Dorsey's.

In his magazine, Watson wrote,

> "Far and wide, the accusation has been strewn, that we [Southerners] are prejudiced against this young libertine [Frank], because he is a Jew. If there is such a racial dislike of the Hebrews among us, why is it that, in the formation of the Southern Confederacy, we placed a Jew in the Cabinet, and kept him there to the last? Why is

it, we are constantly electing Jews to the State legislatures, and to Congress?"

[*Watson's magazine*, Jan. 1915]

Given all these facts we can very firmly establish several concrete truths. Frank lied, often, during the trial. Frank had motive to do the deed, namely, perverse lecherousness, which, once rebuked, reacted with fury that eventually resulted in the murder. Only Frank could possibly have killed Mary Phagan since, as previously stated, he was the only one in the factory at the time who had an enclosed and segregated space to do such a deed unobserved and he later admitted that he had "unconsciously" gone into the very room where Phagan had been murdered. Additionally, anti-Semitism clearly was not the driving force for the case, especially not in the philo-Semitic, Christian South (devout Christians, after all, typically tend to view Jews as fellow people of the Good Book and as God's chosen). For instance, when the aforementioned prosecutor, Hugh Dorsey, made his remarks about Frank shaming his lofty Jewish ancestors, he was greeted with cheers by the locals once he emerged from the court house for the day which is clearly not the sort of thing you would expect out of a bunch of irrationally heated Jew haters. What "anti-Semite" would cheer for someone who was defending the honor of the Jewish people?

Frank was, in no uncertain terms, a sexual deviant, guilty of the hideous crime; for the great heft of the vast bulk of all the evidence was and is against him. This, the researchers at the ADL know very well, just as they likely knew it at the time, yet despite the obvious, they have maintained Frank's innocence for over 100 years, all to protect their reputation – who, after all, would take the Anti-Defamation League at their word if they knew the truth that the ADL was founded on a grievous lie?

Chapter II

THE ADL VS. HENRY FORD (1915-1933)

Shortly after the ADL's formation and the close of the Frank Case, war reared its ugly head – World War I, the first "great war" of the industrialized age, had begun. 52-year-old automotive industrialist and beloved American icon, Henry Ford, upon hearing of the continental strife, was horrified. A pacifistic man by nature, Ford abhorred war; during that time oft remarking how wasteful and hideous the whole affair was. He noted to the *Detroit Free Press* that American armament creation was "wasteful and war-breeding." But Ford was not a man who let things pass him by and so sought to rectify the situation by sailing out to Europe in protest on a "peace ship." The idea for the venture had come from a Hungarian Jew and idealistic suffragette named Rosika Schwimmer who Ford, a liberal, supported for her stalwart opposition to the war. With the cry of, "*We're going to get the boys out of the trenches by Christmas!*" Ford set off to Europe on the Scandinavian-American ship *Oscar II* to mediate the belligerent continental powers – yet before the departure an incident occurred which so outraged Schwimmer that she would later proclaim it "cheap and vulgar." What induced such emotions in the feminist-crusader was a series of proclamations made by Mr. Ford during a conversation pertaining to the root-cause(s) of the war; Ford said, *"I know who caused the war – the German-Jewish bankers. I have the evidence here,"* the industrialist slapped his pocket triumphantly, *"Facts. I can't give them out yet because I haven't got them all. But I'll have them soon."*

When the War ended in 1918, Henry Ford commissioned his private secretary, Ernest Gustav Leibold to purchase *The Dearborn Independent* (later it would also be known as *The Ford International Weekly*) from the previous owner, Marcus Woodruff who had been operating the company at a loss. The used press for the publication was ensconced in the now famous Rouge River Factory in Dearborn, Michigan, the area from which the publication derived its name. Ford maintained several of the key figures of the previous staff such as E.G. Pipp and a former Detroit news writer, William J. Cameron who would write the column known as *Mr. Ford's Page*, in addition to many of the seminal pieces in the paper's canon.

One year later, as the *Independent*'s publication formally began under its new owner, Ford took a camping trip with his good friends, Harvey Firestone, founder of Firestone Tire and Rubber Company, John Burroughs the renowned essayist and naturalist, and Thomas Alva Edison, the "Wizard of Menlo Park."

Burroughs recalled in his diaries that during the meeting of these great men Ford spoke a good deal about "the Jews" and their relation to the War. When Edison remarked upon the decline of the United States navy Ford promptly noted that Jewish meddling had brought about this particularly unhappy deficiency. Somewhat later, at the Ford Motor Company, an executive would find Mr. Ford alone at night, the two striking up a conversation which turned to the "Peace Ship" voyage. The executive asked Ford what he had gotten out of the venture which had ostensibly been a total failure, both in terms of its intended effects and in terms of public perception. Ford responded in a mysterious, knowing fashion,

"I know who makes the wars – the international Jewish bankers arrange them so they can make money out of them." He further added, *"I know it's true because a Jew on the Peace Ship told me... That man knew what he was talking about – gave me the whole story. We're going to tell the whole story one of these days and show them up!"*

It was a statement that would prove quite prophetic, for in 1920, Ford issued forth a striking, inflammatory piece in his now well-syndicated publication titled, *The International Jew: The World's Foremost Problem*. A section of the article reads as follows,

"*The Jew is again being singled out for critical attention throughout the world. His emergence in the financial, political and social spheres has been so complete and spectacular since the war, that his place, power and purpose in the world are being given a new scrutiny, much of it unfriendly. Persecution is not a new experience to the Jew, but intensive scrutiny of his nature and super-nationality is. He has suffered for more than 2,000 years from what may be called instinctive anti-Semitism of the other races, but this antagonism has never been intelligent nor has it been able to make itself intelligible. Nowadays, however, the Jew is being placed, as it were, under the microscope of economic observation that the reasons for his power, the reasons for his separateness, the reasons for his suffering may be defined and understood. In Russia he is charged with being the source of Bolshevism, an accusation which is serious or not according to the circle in which it is made; we in America, hearing the fervid eloquence and perceiving the prophetic ardor of young Jewish apostles of social and industrial reform, can calmly estimate how it may be. In Germany he is charged with being the cause of the Empire's collapse and a very considerable literature has sprung up, bearing with it a mass of circumstantial evidence that gives the thinker pause. In England he is charged with being the real world ruler, who rules as a super-nation over the nations, rules by the power of gold, and who plays nation against nation for his own purposes, remaining*

himself discreetly in the background. In America it is pointed out to what extent the elder Jews of wealth and the younger Jews of ambition swarmed through the war organizations – principally those departments which dealt with the commercial and industrial business of war, and also the extent to which they have clung to the advantage which their experience as agents of the government gave them."
[*The Dearborn Independent*, issue 12, June, 1920]

The basic thesis of the sum-total text was that a largely monolithic cabal of Jewish banksters from various different countries, including America, France, England and Germany, had schemed in such a fashion so as bring about the first World War for the purposes of financial gain and their own group's ethnic and political advancement and were now scheming to do as much again.

Ford had four paperbacks, feature-length books published via the Dearborn Publishing Company concerning Jewish influence, those being *The International Jew: The World's Foremost Problem* (1920), *Jewish Activities in the United States* (1921), *Jewish Influences in American Life* (1921) and lastly, *Aspects of Jewish Power in the United States* (1922). These various volumes are sometimes all colloquially referred to as *The International Jew: The World's Foremost Problem* and were widely distributed in various versions and languages, both in the US and further abroad.

Despite being a success, the volumes and articles rather predictably whipped up a fervor within the Jewish community and those who sympathized with them. It was a push-back which Ford had predicted when, in *The International Jew*, William J. Cameron (who penned the majority of the Jewish-critical pieces) wrote,

"In simple words, the question of the Jews has come to the fore, but like other questions which lend themselves to prejudice, efforts will be made to hush it up as impolitic for open discussion. If, however, experience has taught us anything it is that questions thus suppressed will sooner or later break out in undesirable and unprofitable forms."
[*The Dearborn Independent*, issue 12, June, 1920]

It was a statement that would prove all too accurate, as the articles were widely circulated (*The Dearborn Independent* had a peak circulation of around 700,000, though some sources place it at 900,000) and also widely read and trusted (especially by European Americans), due to Ford's popularity as an affable captain of industry and champion of the working man – indeed, it would not be hyperbolic to say that Ford, during the 1920s was one of the best-loved and respected men in all of America. Ford was also one of the richest with a vertically integrated company worth billions (around $199 billion, to be precise). He ingeniously engineered cars in such a fashion so as to make them available to the common man, rather than mere playthings of the ultra-rich, as they had been since their inception. Despite his esteem and monumental accomplishments, not everyone was pleased with the industrialist's work, especially not the Jewish-American community who swiftly began boycotting his products and sending letter after letter of vitriolic complaint to Ford. The most egregiously aroused of these poison-penners consisted of the National Council of Jewish Women, the Central Conference of American Rabbis as well as the still very active B'nai B'rith, whose current chair was the league's founder and prominent attorney, Sigmund Livingston.

Outraged that Ford and his agents were able to freely disseminate their "anti-Semitic" opinions, these incensed organizations pooled their efforts and sought out the Anti-Defamation League, demanding prompt and decisive action. The ADL readily agreed that something should be done about the Jewish-critical articles and set itself into a vigorous contemplation of how best to shut down the publication and tarnish Ford's reputation as well as his various employees and associates. The League's first course of action was to set forth a pamphlet entitled, *The Poison Pen*, which harshly criticized the *Dearborn Independent*. The ADL's actions were incredibly effective, so much so that shortly after the publication of *The Poison Pen*, then-President Woodrow Wilson, as well as former presidents, Taft and Roosevelt and William Jennings Bryan, along with other prominent and ostensibly respectable individuals, signed a paper titled, *The Perils of*

Racial Prejudice. The tract vociferously denounced *The Dearborn International* and vehemently urged public opinion-makers to "strike at" the "un-Christian" and "un-American" publication. All of the signees were notable in that they were all gentiles, that is, non-Jews, they were also all Christians. Continuing on this theme, the Michigan publication was also denounced by the now defunct religious coalition known as the Federal Council of Churches, an ecumenical Protestant organization comprised of thirty-two different Christian sub-denominations.

Presidents, present and former, and ardent Judeo-Christians, however, were not the only ones to take aim at the publication and Ford himself; the well-known lawyer, Samuel Untermeyer wrote that *The International Jew* read as if it had been penned by a madman and additionally remarked that the piece had become "the Bible of every anti-Semite."

Despite the increasing ferocity and frequency of the press vitriol against him and his paper, Ford did not back down and instead, continued on with his publications against "International Jewry" (it is here of note that during this time Jews themselves utilized the phrase "Jewry," generally in a positive communal sense).

Eventually, Ford's social efforts turned toward the Jewish-lead agricultural cooperation movement and its relationship to American husbandry. The movement was helmed by a man named Aaron Sapiro, a Jewish lawyer and political activist who had received notoriety in 1923 and 1924 for several prominent speeches he had given in the States and the Canadian Provinces, principally, Saskatchewan. Despite his humble origins, short stature (his growth had been stunted from malnutrition) and relatively low social standing, Sapiro's intelligence, idealism and magnetic charisma inspired both popularity and loyalty. After years of giving numerous speeches concerning agricultural reform and progressive social issues all about the states, Sapiro began coordinating what came to be known as "The Sapiro Plan," which advocated for agricultural cooperatives that would focus on commodity-specific strategies rather than on territory specific strategy, ideas which were initially espoused by his mentor, Dave Lubin who was a key player in the internationalization of American markets at the time.

In April, 1924, the former rabbinical student, Sapiro, became aware of the *Independent*'s section titled, "*Jewish Exploitation of the American Farmer's Organizations: Monopoly Traps Operate Under the Guise of Marketing Associations*," which was featured in *The International Jew*. The piece mentioned Sapiro by name and harshly criticized him and various other Jewish co-op advocates. One section of the piece noted that Sapiro's meddling had "*turned millions away from the pockets of the men who till the soil and into the hands of the Jews and their followers.*" Sapiro, a rather ill-tempered and vengeful man, took Ford to court for libel in 1925, in a federal district court in Chicago. Ford happily obliged despite concerns from his right-hand man Liebold who had, until this time, been the foremost champion of the paper's Jewish-critical efforts.

Now the trial itself and its principal players bear some deliberation as it was a most curious affair, especially where Sapiro is concerned, for the historical narrative here gets rather polemical. Upon looking the case up online one (especially on the ADL's website) is given the impression of a wholly one-sided play, with Aaron Sapiro playing a near-helpless yet heroically tenacious, almost messianic figure, fighting against the defamation of his people and Ford assuming the role of a cartoonishly malevolent (or sometimes incompetent) big-money bigot who simply can't wait to crush "the little guy."

Obviously, things were a bit more subtle and complicated than all that. One of the people who has done the utmost to bring this particular piece of history to the fore is the research professor for the American Bar Association of Chicago, Victoria Saker Woeste. Ms. Woest has done much work concerning the history of Ford's legal disputes, typified in her most recent book upon the subject titled, *Henry Ford's War on Jews and the Legal Battle for Hate Speech* (2016). From the title alone one understands immediately that Ms. Woeste is, despite her claims to the contrary, engaging in a highly polemical exercise that is painting Ford as a villain from the outset. It is clear that her work is biased from the start against Ford and upon listening to her speak or reading her work one quickly realizes that she has great admiration for Sapiro which is understandable given his accomplishments and obvious intellectual gifts for organization, rhetoric and agricultural innovation.

That being said, Sapiro was no saint and neither was he, as Woeste describes him "a nobody from California." In fact, by 1925, Sapiro had amassed around 890,000 farmers from all across the nation into his cooperative network. *The New York Times* described him as "the leader of one of the greatest agricultural movements of modern times." Clearly Sapiro was not some random roustabout, not "the little guy" or average Joe, but rather quite a powerful figure, which is not to say that one should hold this fact against him (or Ford, for that matter) but the issue should be clearly and factually stated to better understand the context of what was next to transpire.

Sapiro went for broke and sued Ford for $1 million in damages – to put this sum in its proper historical context, then-president Calvin Coolidge was earning only $75,000 a year! Sapiro also went further, claiming that Ford had not just libeled him, personally, but that the auto-tycoon had also libeled the whole Jewish race. Unfortunately, for Sapiro, the case in question concerned only Ford and Sapiro himself meaning that any comments pertaining to anyone other than Sapiro were inadmissible since hate speech legislation had not, at this point in time, been wholly instantiated within America's legal infrastructure. Furthermore, Louis Marshall, a famous lawyer and Jewish civil rights leader who had been brought into the case by a friend of Ford's named Earl Davis, was none too keen on Sapiro's ethnocentric appeals. Marshall, though a supporter of the Balfour Declaration and the then-president of the American-Jewish Committee, never involved himself in cases pertaining to "anti-Semitism." Instead, Marshall (who had staunchly opposed Sapiro's libel suit from the start) wanted to settle the suit in a way that would benefit all parties involved without overt appeals to ethnocentricity (though, it should be said, Marshall very much wanted things to end in manner which would benefit the Jewish community). To this end Marshall extended his help to Ford under one condition, that the industrialist repudiate his infamous work, *The International Jew* – this despite the fact that Sapiro's suit against Ford had absolutely nothing to do with the whole of the publication, but merely a 1924 addition of the paper which mentioned Sapiro by name.

Ford was stretched thin at this point in time given that his new Model A car was slated to be released very soon, additionally he had been run off the road (allegedly) during the course of the trial and may have feared for his life, thus, he readily agreed to Marshall's plan and allowed a letter to be written which denounced his previous works and praised the Jewish peoples. Upon Marshall's publication of "Ford's" letter of apology (which Ford did not write nor sign) the Jewish community (for the most part) praised him. Sapiro was not convinced that his wily foe was truly repentant but decided that he had accomplished all that he had wanted

– Sapiro's legal expenses were also quite considerable, which was another factor which doubtless played into his acquiescence of the apology.

Ford himself, never apologized for the affair nor did he ever see the note of apology according to one of his closest associates, a Jew named Harry Bennett (who signed the Marshall apology). Indeed, Bennet wrote a whole book concerning the affair and Ford more generally, entitled, *Ford: We Never Called Him Henry* (1950).

Ford and Sapiro reached an out-of-court settlement in 1927. On December the 31st of that same year Henry Ford would close up *The Dearborn Independent* for good.

Ford was perhaps the most illustrious and well known of the ADL's targets and one who, in life, they were never able to defeat. Yet in death, the organization continues to defame the great industrialist even as they (begrudgingly) sing his well-earned praises. For instance, in a bevy of articles published to the ADL's main web-page they consistently mention Ford's name in connection with a host of disreputable trouble makers, such as the Nation of Islam's vociferous racialist preacher, Louis Farrakhan who has, in the past, made a number of bizarre, empirically unverified or unverifiable statements such as, "*You* [black people] *are not now, nor have you ever been a citizen of America. You are a slave to white America,*" he has also made the peculiar remark that, "*The Mother Wheel is a heavily armed spaceship the size of a city, which will rain destruction upon white America but save those who embrace the Nation of Islam."* For the purposes of clarification, Farrakhan meant the latter comment literally. Regardless of your opinion of Farrakhan, the ADL's constant mentioning of Ford in proximity to Farrakhan seems to be a way in which to say, "Look, if you criticize ethnocentric Jews you'll end up believing in Mother Wheels and demons!" This conclusion is somewhat speculative, I will admit, so let us turn our attention to the more fundamental and more empirically demonstrable issue – Ford's supposed "anti-Semitism."

Was Mr. Ford an "anti-Semite?" Well before we can answer that question we must accurately define our terms. Taken literally, anti-Semite seems to mean someone who is opposed to all Semites – that is to say, to all who speak a Semitic language. The problem here is that this definition would include a large array of other ethnic and religious groups, such as Arabs who, in turn, are merely a people who speak Arabic. One never hears Muslim-critical speech defined as "anti-Semitic" nor are the originators of such speech ever described as "anti-Semites." Clearly, the phrase anti-Semite is not, in common parlance, meant to be taken literally, which, in my opinion, is highly unfortunate as any word which has multiple non-literal meanings gains the troublesome attribute of identity-amorphism, that is to say, it seems to be a thing when one wishes it to be a thing and not, when one does not.

Given that we are talking primarily about the ADL, let us turn our attention to their definition of "anti-Semitism" for the purposes of further clarification. According to the ADL, anti-Semitism is defined as:

> *The belief or behavior hostile toward Jews just because they are Jewish. It may take the form of religious teachings that proclaim the inferiority of Jews, for instance, or political efforts to isolate, oppress, or otherwise injure them.*
>
> *It may also include prejudiced or stereotyped views about Jews.*

Now this definition is, in fact, even more broad then the literal definition of the term. For where it says, "to isolate, oppress, or otherwise injure them," we must ask who is the "them" to which they are referring? Even though the ADL itself oft complains when any individual looks upon the whole of the Jewish peoples as a monolith, this seems to be, here, precisely what they are doing. That being said, let us see if the ADL's definition, poor and amorphous as it is, applies to Ford himself.

Certainly Ford did not consider ALL Jews a monolith, for the very title of his book, *The International Jew*, attests to this very fact. Whether you think he was largely correct or largely incorrect as regards his (and Cameron's and Liebold's) theories about this international group is irrelevant to whether or not he believed ALL of the Jewish people acted ever in concert. If Ford really was opposed to ALL Jews in uniformity he simply would have named the book "The Jew," leaving aside the descriptor "International." In addition to this, we must also consider the fact that Ford had many Jewish friends and employed thousands of Jews at his factories (which he paid just the same as any of his other employees). Ford himself was shocked at the vitriolic outrage he received from some of his Jewish friends after the publication of his papers, yet many of those very same friends remained by his side all throughout the car-king's battles with Hollywood, the ADL, Sapiro and various international forces. In fact, Ford was so fond of one of his Jewish friends, a popular rabbi named Leo Franklin, that once, every year, the industrialist would send him a brand new car – free – as a show of appreciation. Yet, once Ford and Cameron began publishing their Jewish-critical pieces, and the next year came, Franklin rejected the car, telling the driver, "I can't accept that." Ford, confused and concerned, called his friend, asking, "Rabbi, has something come between us?" Franklin responded, "Yeah, you're attacking Jews. I can't accept anything from you." Ford responded matter-of-factly, "No, I'm not attacking Jews, I'm attacking bad Jews. I would think you'd be supportive of that."

The rabbi wrote of *The Dearborn Independent*'s articles,

> "Such venom could only come from a Jew-hater of the lowest type, and here it was appearing in a newspaper owned and controlled by one whom the Jews had counted among their friends. It was veritably a bolt out of the blue."

THE ADL VS. HENRY FORD

Henry Ford and the Jews: The Mass Production of Hate, Neil Baldwin (2003)

Despite the rabbi's misgivings, and obvious sense of disappointment and resentment, he and Ford eventually patched up their relationship and remained fast-friends until Franklin's death in the late 40s. Additionally, Ford was also considered, both at the time and in modern-day publications by most liberal thinkers to be "ahead of his time" on race and gender issues (so long as they were not race and gender issues related to Jews). For instance, Ford employed both women and blacks at a time when very few other companies would – not only that, but he also paid them the exact same wage as his white, male workers.

In his book, *Henry Ford and the Jews: The Mass Production of Hate*, the cultural historian, Neil Baldwin writes that Ford's social views were indicative of an "almost bipolar trait." Yet there is nothing "bipolar" about dichotomizing any given ethnic group into *good* and *bad* categories so long as the distinctions made are accurate. Such a principal holds regardless of whether one disagrees or agrees with Ford and Cameron's conclusions. Indeed, the United States government does as much to this very day, they merely do not call it as such; for why would a government note race-&-religion in crime statistics if those who compiled them were not interested in mapping out and dichotomizing said groups along such lines as good and bad individuals? The answer is clear, they would not, for unlike a think-tank, the government is not collecting such information merely for academic purposes but for future enforcement of law and the safeguarding of their interests. Additionally, many of the Jewish groups which Baldwin seems to think were horribly maligned were doing precisely what he criticizes Ford for (in that many Jews considered Ford to be a bad Euro-American) – were they "bipolar?" I shall not put words in anyone's mouth – one would have to ask Mr. Baldwin to be sure – but it doesn't seem a stretch to assume his answer would be a resounding, "No." At this point I am hopeful that the reader will discern that Ford, though he certainly made mistakes, was not the ignorant, hateful schizoid who so many scholars seem to make him out to be; nor was he an "anti-Semite" even by the ADL's own proffered definition of the very word.

Popular opinion held that Ford was the loser of the affair, albeit a fairly gracious one and Aaron Sapiro the victor. Such sentiments, however, betrayed the truth of the matter and all that was later to transpire for the libel case had nearly bankrupted Sapiro who had moved from New York City to Chicago where he was warmly embraced by the Jewish community. More damaging than that, however, was a series of incidents in Chicago that seem to lend some credence to the claims that Ford and William J. Cameron laid out against the Jewish lawyer. On July 28th 1933, Aaron Sapiro was implicated in a Chicago-based racketeering scheme alongside none other than crime boss Al Capone as well as

Capone's likely heir, Murray Humphreys. *The Michigan Daily* describes the event thusly,

Chicago's War on Gangsters

NEW YORK, July 27. (AP) – Aaron Sapiro was taken to Police Headquarters late today, charged with being a fugitive from Chicago, where he was indicted on a charge of racketeering conspiracy.

CHICAGO, July 27. (W) – Reputable attorneys and industrial arbiters, labor union bosses, plain hoodlums and Al Capone himself were named alike in a blanket indictment today, charging 24 men with bombing, acid-throwing and restraint of legitimate trade through terrorism. Eminent among the defendants were:

• AARON SAPIRO, New York attorney, who once sued Henry Ford for $1,000,000. He is a pioneer organizer of the co-operative marketing movement in the United States, named because he was counsel for nearly a year of the Chicago Laundry Owners Association. He quit June 2.

• DR. BENJAMIN M. SQUIRES, University of Chicago lecturer on economics, Federal labor mediator who was appointed head of the Master Cleaners and Dyers Institute of Chicago for the announced purpose of eradicating the gangsters.

• ALDERMAN OSCAR NELSON, Republican leader of the City. Council, attorney for the Dye House Drivers Union.

• AL CAPONE, who might still be the czar of Chicago's outlaw labor rackets, ruling by the gun, had the Government not put him in prison for 11 years on an income tax evasion conviction.

• MURRAY HUMPHREYS, successor to Capone as Public Enemy No. 1, business boss of the syndicate, a fugitive now from Federal indictments charging that he dodged his income tax bill.

Sapiro was acquitted of the charges, namely, labor racketeering, but then again, so were all of the 22 defendants, several of whom were then well known criminals, chief among which is notorious Chicago-based, prohibition era crime boss, Al Capone. It should also be noted that Sapiro's freedom was only assured after the Illinois attorney general killed himself. Let us also note that Sapiro's affiliation to syndicated crime lends some credibility here to Ford and Cameron's assertion's over shady dealings and plans. There is also the fact that Dave Lubin and Sapiro's plans would have effectively cornered the wheat market across international lines, which, regardless of intentions, was something which wasn't at all irrational to oppose.

Regardless of whether Sapiro was guilty of the racketeering scheme, his agricultural plan would have done nearly everything which Cameron and Ford accused him of – the principal question here is merely of motivation, was it nefarious or benign? That is a matter still of historical dispute and thus I shall not take pains here to answer it and leave it up to the reader to decide. Instead, I wish to redirect our attention, for Sapiro was not the only one who was indicted on charges of a racketeering scheme (which he may, or may not have been a part of) he also had a very close association with a man whose name conjures up the blackest of villainy.

Meyer Lansky.

Yet Sapiro was the least of the players involved in the Ford affair who were connected to organized crime; the most prominent of them all was none other than the ADL itself.

Chapter III

WWII & THE ADL MAFIA
(1933-1985)

At the same time Henry Ford was struggling with the financial instability brought about by the great banking collapse of 1933, a plethora of gangster's breathed a sigh of relief as prohibition came to an end. One of these men was Morris "Moe" Barney Dalitz, who, in large part, made Las Vegas what it is today – he was also one of the most powerful gangster's in American history whose legacy of bootlegging, racketeering and shadowy influence still reverberates throughout US history to this very day.

Dalitz was born in Boston in December 24th, 1899, to a gambling father who ran a humble industrial laundry outfit. When Morris was still a babe his father moved the family to Ann Arbor, Michigan. It was there that Dalitz began his myriad criminal enterprises, starting with his affiliation to the Detroit terrorizing Purple Gang who rose to prominence after the establishment of the 1916 Damon Act (or Damon Law) which outlawed the sale of alcohol in Michigan. The Act made Michigan one of the first "dry" states, thus paving the way for an underground liquor trade which was well underway when Prohibition was established nationally in 1920. The Purple Gang was a loose confederation of Jewish toughs who delighted in hijacking motorcars along the frigid Lake St. Clair and gunning down all unfortunate souls therein. The gang was also well known for their racketeering, shakedowns and strong-arm kidnappings (they were even implicated in the kidnapping and murder of 20-month old Charles A. Lindbergh, Jr., the son of famed aviator, Charles Lindbergh). The Purples were so ruthless that current estimates state that they killed approximately 500 of their rivals during their brief reign as kings of the Detroit Underground. It was with these bloodstained criminals that Moe Dalitz struck up a business partnership (though he was never formally a member), primarily in the shipment of illegal hooch. This alliance was driven by Dalitz's friendship with the leader of the Purple Gang, Abe Bernstein, a powerful and ruthless Jewish gangster from Detroit who would later go on to help Al Capone in his efforts to eliminate his archrival-in-crime, Bugs Moran.

After the repeal of the oft-disregarded Volstead Act in 1933, Dalitz, unlike many of his co-criminals, determined that post-Prohibition America would increase the demand for bootlegged spirits, rather than decrease it. Dalitz came to this conclusion due to the fact that, though liquor was now legal again, the government was still determined that sales thereof should be reduced as much as possible through increased taxation and various legislative actions. To this end, in November of 1933, Dalitz (then utilizing the name Davis) and several confederates founded a company called Molaska. His benefactors and friends at the time were a venerable rogues-gallery of disrepute, including such big-time mafiosi as Salvatore "Lucky" Luciano and math whiz and Murder Inc. architect, Meyer Lansky, who was represented via proxy by his father-in-law, Moses Citron. Both Lansky and Luciano had been mentored by the late Arnold "The Brain" Rothstein, the Jewish criminal who had pioneered bootlegging-as-a-major-business in conjunction with the British government and the Bronfman Family (Seagram Company) during Prohibition. Other notable associates of Dalitz's at the time included Jewish mob-man, Abner "Longie" Zwillman and Italian gangster and long-time friend of Luciano, Frank "The Prime Minister" Costello.

Lansky (born Meier Suchowlański) met Luciano when they were teenagers with the headstrong Italian attempting to extort some money from the smallish Jew. Lansky, however, was unintimidated; Luciano was impressed by his tenacity and guts and shortly thereafter, they forged a friendship that would last a lifetime and along the way, laid the foundations for one of the most profitable and powerful criminal syndicates in American history. Lansky had known the Citron family since he was a child and, in 1930, he married Anna Citron,

Moses' daughter. The marriage was not an especially happy one but Lansky and Moses developed a firm friendship, so much so that the elder Citron never asked the Jewish mobster how exactly he made ends meet. Due to this familial relationship, Moses invested $120,000 in Dalitz's Molaska venture, which was a tremendous sum, especially considering the financial destabilization of the times which had been brought about by the Great Depression. 1000 shares of Moses Citron's investment were then given to his attorney to be held in trust.

The attorney's name was Aaron Sapiro, the very same man who had sued auto-magnate Henry Ford for libel some years earlier, the very same man who is lauded by the ADL to this day. Sapiro had also participated in the violent Dryers and Cleaners Wars along with Italian crime-boss and bootlegging overlord, Al Capone. Though both men were indicted, neither Capone nor Sapiro were convicted of anything.

Molaska itself was, ostensibly, a company that produced molasses for use in animal food. Molaska's true function, however, was as an illegal alcohol distillery producing whiskey and beer which were surreptitiously crafted and shipped all around the country by truck.

Robert Bridges, a government investigator who worked under famous Prohibition special agent, Elliot Ness, began looking into Molaska and discovered a number of curiosities, namely that the building remained constantly under lock and key and that a guard could ever be seen walking the property.

He also noticed that strange fumes could be seen coming from the company property during the Winter months – alcohol fumes combined with steam – a sight every former Prohibition agent knew exceedingly well. Despite the Bridges' investigation, and others, Dalitz and Lansky's plans remained undisturbed and exceedingly profitable. In 1935 the Molaska partners decided to file for bankruptcy and swindle the system. Not long after this occurred, Molaska was reconstituted and the various operators shifted away, taking their earnings with them.

Several years later, in 1939, the National Socialist German army enacted the Fall Weiss and invaded Poland and initiated the second great intercontinental struggle of the modern age. World War II. At this time, in America, the rambunctious and pro-Reich and anti-Roosevelt German-American Bund (*Amerikadeutscher Volksbund*) party was at the height of their power. The group had first been formed in Buffalo, New York, 1936, as a successor movement to FONG, (Friends of New Germany movement). The Volksbund was led by a German-American named Fritz Julius Kuhn who formed a close alliance with the notorious preacher, Charles Coughlin (a notable promoter of Ford's *The International Jew*), and leader of the Christian Front.

The German-American Bund was notorious for their gaudy marches and fiery speeches, usually headed by Kuhn himself wherein he oft echoed National Socialist Germany's disdain for Jewry

(Kuhn once referred to Roosevelt's New Deal as "The Jew Deal") and also expressed and championed international white (particularly German) solidarity.

Lansky, who despite his foul reputation and utter disregard for the laws of the land, considered himself something of a patriot, a "true American." More than that, Lansky, a fervent Zionist, possessed a deep sense of ethnic pride and was outraged at the widely publicized plight of his fellow Eastern European Jews upon the continent. Due these loyalties, Lansky attempted to enlist in the United States army to fight against Germany but was turned down due to his short height (he stood only five-foot, four-inches tall) and age (40). Lansky, however, would not be deterred and so turned to the assistance of a personal friend and neighbor named Walter Winchell. Winchell was, at the time, one of, if not THE, most influential journalist in all of America. The secret to his influence, at least in part, was due a close personal relationship with then-president Roosevelt, who at the time was exceedingly concerned about saboteurs. These fears only deepened when, on the 9th of February, 1942, the French luxury liner, SS Normandie caught fire as it was being converted into a battle carrier for the war effort. First-hand reports stated that an acetylene torch had cause the inferno but some amongst the admiralty smelled a rat – a German scented one. The US Naval office, under the auspices of daring Commander Charles Haffenden, grew wary of Fascist and "Nazi" apparatchiks and decided to enlist the help of a crook by the name of Joseph Lanza – known in the streets as "Socks" due to his proclivity for punching anyone who displeased him – a member of the murderous and exceedingly powerful Genovese Crime Family. Haffenden turned to this particular criminal primarily because Lanza controlled the whole of Manhattan's Fulton Fish Market, an important strategic area in the Navy's fight against Fascist and National Socialist infiltrators and saboteurs. Though a fishmonger might not sound like a particularly powerful ally, Lanza's mundane trade belied his savage nature. With a criminal history stretching back all the way to 1917, including extortion, battery, racketeering, conspiracy and murder, "Socks" Lanza was not a man to be trifled with. Despite his cantankerous nature, "Socks" Lanza jumped at the opportunity to aid the Navy against the Fascists which placed Commander Haffenden in the peculiar position as something of a US sanctioned mob boss. Lanza and his minions proved quite effective at first and, through a number of black-bag operations, helped the Navy uncover numerous German espionage rings. But Lanza's reach had its limits and he and his outfit alone simply couldn't secure the whole of the Brooklyn's seaside territory. Lanza was revered by the Genovese Crime family but was widely detested by the other four crime families which made up the multi-ethnic National Crime Syndicate that ruled the American underworld at the time. One of the other big players who controlled local territory included Albert Anastasia who ran much of the

Mafia murder squad at the behest of Meyer Lansky and Lucky Luciano. Anastasia also controlled the International Longshoreman's Association (ILA) which was of key strategic importance to Haffenden's plans. Unlike many other underbosses, Anastasia often participated directly in mob killings. His blood-thirst earned him the grim moniker "The High Lord Executioner." Lanza feared Anastasia and knew others did as well but he also realized that neither of the two of them, even put together, could move the whole of the docks. Lanza told Haffenden that there was only one man who was capable of "snapping the whip" on the whole of the New York underworld.

Lucky Luciano. The architect of the National Crime Syndicate and leader of the Genovese Family. There was just one problem.

Luciano was on ice.

Serving a 30-50-year sentence in Dannemora Prison (today known as the Clinton Correctional Facility) on numerous counts of prostitution, the scar-faced Italian scion – though still highly respected by The Syndicate which he had created – was in no position to snap the whip on the NYC underbelly; he was too isolated to be giving commands or receiving much information. He needed to be brought into the Navy's fold, but Haffenden knew the mafioso would be suspicious and wouldn't exactly jump at the prospects of working for the very institutions that had put him behind bars. Haffenden needed an intermediary. In Meyer "The Little Man" Lansky, he found one.

Unlike with Lanza, Luciano and Al Anastasia, Haffenden knew Lansky's ethnic-tribal loyalty could be relied upon. The little Jewish mastermind's regular battles against Julius Kuhn's bombastic German-American Bund storm troopers all across New York City was a testament to this (the Bund were considered a "subversive" organization by the FBI).

Once Lansky brought Luciano into the Naval-dockside enforcement plan the rest of the New York mafia quickly fell into line. Haffenden now had a shadow army and near complete control of New York's docks. German National Socialist and Italian Fascist subversion was nearly impossible and the US war machine was bolstered. But there was a cost to the whole affair, one which is scarcely remarked upon by most historians, that being the murder of countless American citizens by Haffenden's disreputable syndicate agents. One of the syndicate associates under Haffenden's control, a burglar and psychotic Irish killer named John "Cockeye" Dunn, was sent to investigate two suspected German agents. Instead of following orders the crazed Irishman sent them on the mafias often cliched "one way trip." They were never seen alive again. Wiretap recordings on Dunn find the fiend stating remorselessly, "They'll never bother us again." Such instances were far from singular and it should be noted that those two unfortunate souls were only "suspected" subversives. The navy frowned upon extra-judicial killing but Haffenden's hackles certainly weren't raised. If the Mafia were "the bad guys" then the Navy considered the German National Socialists and Fascists "the worse guys."

Dalitz also jumped into the war effort and enlisted in 1943. Unlike his confederate, Lansky, Dalitz was accepted and served as an officer in the Quartermaster Corps doing laundry for NYC, rising rapidly through the ranks.

While Meyer Lansky and Haffenden's shadow army seized control of the New York docks for the naval war-time effort and Dalitz folded shirts, the Anti-Defamation League doled out its own campaign concerning the war.

In October of 1943, a FBI informant named Charles M. Scott, forwarded a most peculiar leaflet to the offices of Bureau agent, Leland V. Boardman. Scott stated that he was concerned about what he called "Semitic propaganda" which he alleged that the little missive contained. The document reads as follows:

SPECIAL NOTICE TO ALL JEWS

The central conference of American rabbis at the 47th American conference, held in New York City, June 26, 1937, declared for, "Exemption of Jews from military service in accordance with the highest interpretation of Judaism." Our Talmud tells us, "When you go to war, do not go as the first but as the last, so that you may return as the first."

Why should we, the only truly international people, be concerned with the mutable interests of stupid goyim nations? We must do everything in our power to help the great president who has helped us so greatly in establishing control. Support the draft law when it is presented to the American people. Support England and France, for they are fighting Judah's greatest enemy, the Goyim German State. You are urged to support United States participation in this Holy War of Judah, without reservation and without fear. We can repeat our triumphs of 1918 if we maintain our united front and the dumb goyim will fight while we profit, with the aid of our friends in Washington.

Powerful Jews will be on all draft boards, and Jewish physicians will protect you from military service. Arrangements are already made to exempt you in case religious exemption cannot be prepared in time.

You are warned to renounce, abjure, repudiate and deny any of this information if questioned by Gentiles, even under oath, as outlined in the Talmud and justified for the preservation of our race.

The Central Committee
Anti-Defamation League BB

At the first, one might begin to feel pinpricks of suspicion, for the language is so unguarded and so over-the-top (i.e. "stupid goyim") that it seems fairly obvious that the letter is a fake. The FBI's criminal investigative unit took a keen interest in the letter and began looking into the affair as a matter of

sedition. A year later, in 1944, the FBI discovered that the very same leaflets had been distributed in June of 1941 in the Cleveland area. This information came to light via the League of Human Rights, a Cleveland (Ohio) based social justice group. The League of Human Rights stated that the document in question was an absolute fake designed to cause ethnic tension. Their reasoning for this was two-fold:
1. The leaflet noted that the 47th Conference of American Rabbis took place upon June 26, 1937 when in reality it took place a year earlier in 1936.
2. Experts hired by The League of Human Rights determined that the typewriter used to create the Semitically propagandizing leaflets was the very same sort of typewriter utilized by the United Mothers of America, a religious/nationalist organization headed up by anti-war and anti-Jewish preacher and political personality, Father Charles Coughlin, a long-time arch-enemy of The League who was the subject of numerous ADL and B'nai B'rith hit-pieces in their subscription publications.

Yet it should also be noted that during the same year that The League of Human Rights discovered the Semitic leaflets in Cleveland, other, identical mimeographed copies, were discovered in Chicago.

Whilst the FBI looked into the puzzling matter of the pejorative papers the Anti-Defamation League looked on and planned its next move.

Scheming over the course of several years, they sent agent after agent to try to worm themselves inside the Federal Bureau of Investigation, the better to get at their stockpile of personal information. Yet their schemes availed them not. They were constantly rebuffed.

FBI internal memorandum from 1943-1944 (mostly from SACs – Special Agents in Charge) clearly displays a certain impatience and exasperation, as well as a growing sense of wariness, towards the ADL. Some previous instances of the oft contentious relationship between the ADL and FBI include a 1940s incident wherein an undercover confederate of The League attempted to block and cover-up the ADL's usage of private investigators from the Bureau and the wider public. The ADL operative stated that, "the Anti-Jewish element has accused the Anti-Defamation League of having private investigators, and the Anti-Defamation League does not wish it to become generally known that they *do* employ private investigators." [emphasis mine] Another more interesting incident occurred two years later in 1942 when P.E. Foxworth, then-head of the FBI's Special Intelligence Service (SIS), the covert counter-intelligence arm of the Bureau, warned the director that the ADL and a group known as the Non-Sectarian Anti-Nazi League were conducting "shake downs" of innocent civilians. Various missives during this period from the ADL also urge the FBI to place less emphasis upon Communist agitators and place more concern upon Fascists and Fascist sympathizers.

DEFAMATION FACTORY

In 1942 the ADL offered the FBI a subscription to their monthly, private publication which was meant only for "key men," *key* here meaning, "helping the ADL." One of the 1942 ADL newsletters provided to the FBI (whose top agents were, at least ostensibly, considered "key men") vigorously defended none other than Meyer Lansky pal, Walter Winchell from a non-too-flattering editorial in *The Cross and the Flag* penned by notorious dissident clergyman, politician and German sympathizer, Gerald L.K. Smith. It should here be noted that Winchell's underworld connections extended far beyond just Lansky, he was also an associate of Owny Madden, one of the most powerful gangsters of the Prohibition era. Winchell also had a close relationship to the FBI, as he was personal friends with acting Bureau director, J. Edgar Hoover and was instrumental in turning over Lansky associate and Murder Inc. member, Lepke Buchalter. In a move of ridiculous superfluousness, the ADL tsk-tsk'd the Bureau for mentioning that Buchalter was "of Jewish extraction" (which he was). When the FBI retorted by saying that it was customary (for obvious pragmatic reasons) to mention the ethnicity and race of a suspect and that they did this for Italians, Germans and Irishmen as much as for Jews the ADL fell silent. Winchell also had a reputation as an extremely vindictive man who attempted to ruin the lives and personal careers of anyone who he just so happened to dislike.

The ADL newsletter described Winchell, in no uncertain terms, as an ally.

However, one of the most shocking and scandalous affairs which the ADL tentacles had slithered into occurred on April 4, 1944 when a letter, likewise dated, reached FBI Special Agent, C.W. Stein. The letter was from Oregon Senator Rufus Holman who had contacted the FBI with complaints concerning a high ranking member of the ADL, a man by the name of David Robinson (head of the local ADL branch) who had created a new organization called the Oregon Defense Committee whose stated purpose was to "help service men." However, Holman noted that the organization did nothing of the kind and was merely an ADL front and that the so called Defense Committee defended no one. Rather, Holman alleged, the ODC (which was really the ADL) went about persecuting anyone and everyone whom they deemed to be "anti-Semitic." Their favored weapon with which to reprimand Oregon-based "anti-Semites" was the boycott which were easy enough to organize given the power of the ADL and Robinson's considerable salary ($10,000 a year). To Holman, the damnedest thing about the whole affair was that the ADL did not state how it came to determine how an individual was "anti-Semitic." He went on to state that the ADL had taken particular exception to him (they considered him to be an "anti-Semite") and that Robinson was attempting to politically railroad him now that Holman was up for reelection. Robinson put all of his social and political weight (and by extension, the weight of the ADL) behind Holman's political opponent, Wayne L. Morse, a former Dean of the University of Oregon Law School. Due this, Holman demanded a sweeping FBI investigation of the ADL.

Special Agent Stein informed Holman that disconcerting as his report happened to be, the ADL did not appear to be in violation of any state statute. Unless some evidence could be provided of a violation or complaint of "subversive" activity no action could be taken. The FBI would not investigate.

Stein then turned to his friend and fellow bureau colleague, David A. Silver. Silver, who was of Jewish extraction himself, was a special agent within the FBI who knew Robinson personally as they both lived in Portland. Stein figured Silver's ethnic outlook as well as his personal connections to the vexing affair would prove insightful. When asked about Robinson, Silver explained that Holman was correct about everything he had said. Robinson was indeed the leader of the local ADL and also had an intensive disdain for Holman whom Robinson believed to be "anti-Semitic." Silver went on to explain that Robinson also believed that Holman was a potential "American fascist" and that Holman was anti-labor and of generally low intelligence. For these reasons, Silver opposed Holman's reelection. Agent Silver also relayed that Robinson was attempting to rally and inveigle the Portland Jewish vote behind Wayne L. Morse, the previously mentioned former Dean of Oregon Law. This corroborated Holman. He wasn't lying. He was being railroaded by The League. The Special Agent also told Stein that two prominent Portland business men of Jewish extraction, Jack Barde and Abe Gilbert respectively, had thrown a dinner for Mr. Holman and were sternly reprimanded by Robinson for their actions (presumably because this indicated very strongly that Holman did not actually have any particular problem with Jews generally speaking which eroded Robinson and the ADL's credibility with the local community – especially its non-Jewish sectors – markedly).

Shortly after the conversation between the two FBI agents concluded, Holman issued another letter to Stein. He had been boycotted by the local Jewish community. It was so bad, according to Holman, that he and his business partner had to close up shop and sell their assets! Holman, unsurprisingly and quite correctly, blamed Robinson and the ADL. He was so furious about the whole affair that he exclaimed he was going to, "Open up on the S.–O.–B.–s!"

Though Holman did indeed "open up" on his detractors, his isolationist positions and soured reputation allowed Wayne Morse to defeat him at the 1944 Oregon senate elections. After his 1944 defeat Holman would never run for public office ever again and would die shortly thereafter.

The ADL had claimed yet another victim.

Though things might not have gone particularly well for Holman, Moe Dalitz was doing just fine after the end of WWII. By 1970s Dalitz was one of the undisputed Kings of Las Vegas. Unlike Lansky, Dalitz had been able to maintain an image of quasi-respectability in his later years to such a degree that many believed he had "gone straight." Dalitz, ever the wily operator, often attempted to aid his rising image by making light about his bootlegging and illegal casino days, once remarking to a friend, "How was I supposed to know those gambling joints were illegal? There were so many judges and politicians in them I figured they had to be alright." He also once glibly remarked to a Senator inquiring about his illicit past, "If you people wouldn't have drunk it, I wouldn't have bootlegged it."

During his time as Vegas big-shot, Dalitz made a great number of charitable contributions to various different, ostensibly righteous organizations. One of the groups to receive significant largess from Dalitz was none other than the Anti-Defamation League of B'nai B'rith. They were pleased and in 1982 awarded Dalitz with the "Torch of Liberty" award – it would have been hard to think of a more ironic title. Dalitz was not alone in making donations to the ADL, many of his co-conspirators and fellow-travelers publicly made fiduciary assistance to The League as well, including lifetime Syndicate members Victor Posner, Meshulam Riklis, Joe Binsey and Edmond Safra.

The ADL was naturally appreciative to the continued largess of the casino-mogul and his rogues-gallery of shadowy friends, so much so that in 1985 the "human rights" organization awarded Dalitz with yet another award, the "Philanthropist of the Year Award." Yet today if you were to search "Moe Dalitz" or "Morris Barney Dalitz" on the ADL's website you'll be treated to a big, fat, nothing, for

Dalitz, as well as any mention of his donations and awards or connections, have been completely scrubbed from the ADL website and shunted down the memory-hole of informational oblivion. At this juncture I was superbly thankful for those programmers responsible for my Snapshot desktop-capture software.

What one man can suppress another can discover.

The truth will out and the truth here is that the ADL, ostensibly a "human rights" organization, was, in no uncertain terms, colluding with killers, thieves, racketeers, flesh-peddlers and all other manner of Jewish-Italian mafiosi.

The interplay, however, between the mob and the ADL ran so deep, in fact, that they even placed Meyer Lansky's daughter on their board of directors!

Chapter IV

POLLARD'S GAMBIT
(1984-1990s)

Jonathan J. Pollard was a peculiar man who harbored strange fantasies. After hearing of the victory of the Six-day War of 1967, at the age of 12, young Jonathan began dreaming of immigrating to Israel. In the Summer of 1971 Pollard was finally able to travel to Israel for a 3-month science camp. He was wholly absorbed with the place. The fixation was to grow to become an all-consuming passion.

In 1972 Pollard attended Standford University.

During Pollard's attendance at Standford many of his colleagues recall him becoming extremely erratic and once even waving a gun around, shouting that people were out to get him. He sometimes also bragged about being a member of the Mossad, though at the time it was obvious that he was not. Around this same time, Pollard became increasingly pro-Israel and seemed extremely interested in doing something meaningful to assist Zion.

In 1979 Pollard entered into service with naval intelligence and – despite being considered rather odd and idiosyncratic by his colleagues – rose to some prominence. He was a studious and highly intelligent individual, considered particularly capable as an information analyst. But he became increasingly concerned with what he perceived as "anti-Israel" sentiments and also came to believe that the US was not providing Israel sufficient informational aid and access.

Through his naval security position Pollard secured a connection with an Israeli intelligence operative in the later period of June, 1984. It was during this period that Pollard was introduced to Col. Aviem Sella, a highly proficient and well known fighter pilot who was, at the time, taking a study leave in the USA. Upon getting to know Sella and realizing that he was as fanatical about Israel as the naval officer himself, Pollard began doling out classified information. The information which Pollard passed to Sella largely concerned military developments in Arab countries. Pollard's dreams were beginning to be realized.

He was now a spy.

But the traitor was but a fledgling spook, having, at this point in the story, only engaged informally with Sella and a few other pro-Israel zealots. His 1984 trip to Paris, however, would change all of that. In November of the same year he was introduced to Sella, Pollard traveled to Paris, France and there was formally brought into the fold of the Israeli spy apparatus. During this covert meeting the newly turned spy was introduced to Rafael Eitan, director of counter-terrorism to then Prime Minister of

Israel and Lehi paramilitary commander, Yitzhak Shamir. Sella was there replaced by the director of covert operations for Shamir, Joseph Yagur, as Pollard's direct handler. During the meeting Pollard's salary was settled upon ($1500 per month) and an over-arching objective established, that being: Dig up as much classified US information as possible on Russian assistance given to Israel's Muslim foes and route it to Israeli apparatchiks. Pollard, who believed that undertaking the mission would help an embattled Israel "win the next war" against the Arabs, heartily agreed and ended his employment with naval intelligence in 1985 at Rafael Eitan's urging, however, his employment for Israel was only beginning.

In the month of January of 85 Pollard would visit the abode of a one Irit Erb once every other week to make deposits of his stolen, often Top-secret, information. Erb was a secretary of the Washington based Israeli Embassy and accepted the caches of reaved data via suitcase. Occasionally, Joseph Yagur would turn up at Erb's apartment to go over the information with Pollard. Yagur was pleased with his minion's work, so much so that Pollard was allotted a significant raise of $1000 (moving his $1500 payouts up to $2500). Yagur also indicated that Pollard's work was known and appreciated by "the highest levels of the Israeli government." Pollard even stopped in to pal around with the Zionist higher-ups in Tel Aviv during July of the same year and stayed there until August. Upon his return, however, various members of the naval intelligence office had become suspicious of their Jewish agent's activity, mainly due to the sheer amount of Arab specific information that Pollard was shifting through. A FBI/NIS investigation swiftly ensued that ended with the Zionist spy's arrest on the 21st of November after a failed Israeli embassy asylum attempt.

The brigand had been caught.

On the very day he was arrested the ADL's NYC headquarters was buzzing like a smoking hornets' nest. Almost immediately after word of Pollard's arrest reached him, ADL Chairman, Kenneth Bialkin jetted off to Israel. The purpose of Bialkin's sudden excursion was to check with Israeli spy apparatchiks in Zion as to the nature of damage control necessary, to acquire assistance and to arrange a legal defense, not just for Pollard but also for the higher ups in the spy ring, such as Aviem Sella who had handled Pollard for the high-tech, Semitic spy-unit, *Lekem*. The tie-ins were fairly obvious, for instance, Sella's wife, Ruth, worked in the ADL's NYC branch as a legal specialist underneath the command of Bialkin.

A CIA probe would later determine that Pollard's activities had placed United States security at significant risk and had also damaged operational efficiency. The financial damage caused by Pollard's spy ring was also astronomical, his work was estimated to have cost the US government billions. The official Central Intelligence documentation on the case states that:

> *"Pollard's espionage has put at risk important US intelligence and foreign-policy interests."*
> [Foreign denial and deception analysis committee. MORI DocID: 1346933]

Pollard pleaded guilty to "conspiracy to commit espionage" on June 5th, 1986 and was subsequently sentenced to life in prison a year later on the 4th of March, 1987. Pollard's wife, Esther Pollard, a co-conspirator who had intimate first-hand knowledge of the affair, was arrested and tried as well. She was sentenced to two concurrent five-year prison terms.

After Pollard's arrest a one Uri Ra'anan, would turn up to state that the Jewish spy was "bright and articulate." It turns out that Uri Ra'anan was a professor who had taught Pollard at the elite Fletcher School of Law and Diplomacy at Tufts University. Ra'anan's personal commentary about Mr. Pollard's personage was fairly banal and unexceptional as it was already well established that, though somewhat neurotic, Pollard was indeed highly intelligent and very well spoken. What was far more interesting was the personal connections which the Ra'anan+Fletcher+Pollard affiliation brought to light. For looking into Pollard's past at Tufts University one finds that one of his classmates at the Fletcher School was none other than Mira Lansky Boland, the granddaughter of the notorious Jewish mafia boss, Meyer Lansky. Ra'anan's closet was not without its share of skeletons either, for he had been involved in an earlier Israeli spy ring in the 1950s & 1960s which focused on surreptitiously recruiting

US businessmen into a European/Russian intelligence circuit. The central hub for Ra'anan's spying operation was the offices of the B'nai B'rith International in Washington, DC. For the duration of the 50s-60s-spy operation, Ra'anan's contact at the B'nai B'rith headquarters was ADL national chairman, Philip Klutznick. Klutznick would later go on to work under the Jimmy Carter Administration, unscathed by his treachery.

The ADL was knee-deep in Pollard stew and yet they escaped the affair with only minor wounds (occasional rumors and the like), yet no indictments and certainly no charges were brought against any of the Pollard-linked ADL officials, not even Bialkin who, with Israeli aid, set up Pollard's defense. The reason for this was the ADL's masterful damage control; for instance, they had firmly asserted that Pollard was dually aligned, that his heart was merely trying to attach itself to two countries at once and that, though he had utterly betrayed his nation, it was only because he truly cared about cementing closer ties between Israel and the US. They also stated, falsely, that Pollard's spying had merely been "friendly espionage." Does such a thing exist? Ask yourself, dear reader, if a close friend betrays your deepest secrets to other personal, business associates, having gathered them surreptitiously, would you still call him a friend?

I certainly wouldn't.

Chapter V

THE ADL VS. LYNDON LAROUCHE

At the same time that Pollard was being placed behind bars the peculiar political figure and Schiller Institute economist, Lyndon H. LaRouche, Jr. was gaining traction. He was already quite well known in America by the 1970s.

1976 brought him much attention for a peculiar TV ad wherein he warned the American public of then-president Jimmy Carter's political advisers, George Ball and Averell Harriman whom LaRouche considered to be "genocidal." By the 1980s he was nationally well known in America, almost a household name. To some LaRouche was a conspiratorially minded kook (he claimed that the rock band, The Beatles, were a British Intelligence psy-op) to others, a brilliant economic analyst and highly original and articulate thinker, writer and orator (as an objective matter he was very well-spoken and produced the prolific magazine *EIR – Executive Intelligence Review*, which, regardless of what one thinks of its opinions, was thoroughly researched).

LaRouche was, in terms of his moral comportment, an exceedingly traditionalist kind of man who loved classical music and decried jazz (also a psy-op, apparently), the violence of single black mothers, British liberalism, sex, drugs and rock-n-roll culture. As regards his political attitudes he was staunchly pro-American, economically international and culturally nationalist, a sort of urbane and gentile proto-Trump. Other contentious views he held were of a decidedly more market-oriented nature, such as his 1980 paper, *America Must Go Nuclear!* wherein LaRouche argued for a US nationwide nuclear energy conversion program. The paper stated:

"On my first day in office, I shall deliver to the Congress a comprehensive energy policy. This legislation will repeal the worst features of the Environmental Protection Act, permitting work to be completed on the approximately 120 nuclear energy plants presently stalled in various phases of construction. It will also provide for the addition of 1,000 gigawatts of nuclear energy by 2000 A.D."

His political views led him into fierce opposition with a multifarious host of power-groups and DC high-fliers, including, Henry A. Kissinger who, at the time, was highly active in Washington, operating under the actor turned President, Ronald Reagan.

They detested each other.

THE ADSL VS. LYNDON LAROUCHE

One of the reasons for Kissinger's animus rested with LaRouche's personal no-holds-barred critiques. For instance, in 1979 LaRouche wrote in his political magazine, *EIR*, that, "Henry A. Kissinger is a raving communist," in 1982 LaRouche released an article entitled, *Kissinger, The Politics of Faggotry*. The piece opens with the line, "*According to a variety of very authoritative sources, Henry A. Kissinger is not a Jew, but a faggot.*" If that wasn't enough, Larouche additionally alleged that Kissinger was a "Soviet Agent."

One can begin to see why Kissinger so detested the man.

LaRouche's hit-pieces became so troublesome to the man that in 1982, Kissinger wrote two letters concerning the rogue economist and sent them to acting FBI Director, William H. Webster.

Kissinger's letter reads:

August 19, 1982

Dear Bill:

I appreciated your letter forwarding the flyer which has been circulated by Lyndon LaRouche, Jr. Because these people have been getting increasingly obnoxious, I have taken the liberty of asking my lawyer, Bill Rodgers, to get in touch with you to ask your advice, especially with respect to security.

It was good to see you at The Grove, and I look forward to the chance to visit again when I am next in Washington.

Warm Regards – Henry A. Kissinger

In addition to Kissinger's circle of political operators another chief opponent of LaRouche and his movement's members was The Anti-Defamation League of B'nai B'rith who initiated a widespread smear campaign against the man, labeling him, in their typical fashion, as "anti-Semitic" for daring to criticize their psychological strong-arm tactics.

January, 1986, U.S. Attorney William Weld joined the fray amidst a slew of slanderous press coverage of LaRouche and his associates. At this time, ADL official, Stuart Lockman boasted that, "ADL is clearly identified as the opponent of the *LaRoucheites* and virtually all of the [negative] public exposure of that group is either ADL produced or generated."

Weld, whose timing couldn't have been better given the media circus, promised to organize and coordinate a prosecutive and investigative effort against LaRouche and company. Attorney Weld's campaign was highly effective for over the next months numerous LaRouche affiliated organizations were banned from various different states including: Caucus Distributors Inc. (fund-raising for organization banned in Alaska, Indiana & Maryland) and Independent Democrats for LaRouche (fund-raising for org. banned in Minnesota).

LaRouche was not, as you might well have guessed by this point, a man to lay back and take this kind of blatant abuse of power and so sued everyone involved in Weld's operation. He sued Weld. He sued the former attorney general, William Smith. He sued the New Jersey bank and Chemical Bank, both of whom had frozen his and his associates' financial assets.

In 1986 The LaRouche Movement's offices in both Virginia and Massachusetts were raided by federal agents including the FBI and IRS as well as various local and state authorities. The raids lasted for two days during which time LaRouche's own personal and heavily guarded estate was surrounded by federal agents. Fearing that the government operatives were going to attempt a groundless home-invasion LaRouche telegrammed President Ronald Regan, stating that any breach of his property in an apprehension attempt, "would be an attempt to kill me. I will not submit passively to such an arrest." He went on to state, "I will defend myself." During the duration of the raids, neither the federal or local authorities made any attempts to gain entry into LaRouche's personal abode.

LaRouche later allayed any fears that he was attempting some kind of Waco-style, hot-box situation by publicly announcing that, should the authorities after him produce a warrant, he and his heavily armed security guards would peaceably comply.

The searches conducted during William Weld's two-day raiding period had yielded nothing but index cards and some notebooks which US Attorney, Henry Hudson, declared had been subpoenaed (required to be submitted to a court of law).

Despite the ostensible lack of any wrong-doing, in 1988, Lyndon LaRouche and six of his close associates were convicted of mail fraud and tax evasion.

"I'm amazed. Absolutely amazed," LaRouche, then 66 years old, stated after the verdict was delivered.

It was the first time in his entire life that Lyndon La Rouche had faced criminal charges. His criminal record was spotless and his manner of conduct was always amicable and peaceful, despite the controversy surrounding his personal opinions. It had been an obvious frame-up job. This isn't merely speculation. There is evidence and it shows just who was at the bottom of it; Henry Kissinger and the ADL.

Kissinger's "Get LaRouche" task force had been very attentively selected and included such notable public figures as newspaper mogul and billionaire, Richard Mellon Scaife, prolific hit-piece writer, Dennis King (who wrote a whole book defaming LaRouche entitled, *Lyndon LaRouche and the New American Fascism*) and, surprise, surprise, Mira Lansky Boland, ADL agent and old friend of Jonathan J. Pollard and student of Israeli spymaster, Uri Ra'anan.

Chapter VI

BULLOCK'S BLUNDER & LAROUCHE'S RETURN

On October the 11th, 1985, Arab activist and Palestinian American, Alex Odeh walked into the offices of the American-Arab Anti-Discrimination Committee, otherwise known as the ADC. As he did so a pipe bomb exploded and killed him. The event was a clear instance of assassination and the murderer would never be found.

In 1987, one year before LaRouche's conviction was handed down, the ADL's longstanding National Chairman, Nathan Pearlmutter, passed away from terminal lung cancer. Pearlmutter was swiftly replaced by the longstanding and highly regarded ADL operative and lawyer, Abraham "The Fox" Foxman. Now the effective czar of the Anti-Defamation League, Foxman, a Zionist supremacist, Armenian genocide denier and anglohater of first rate, doubled up the efforts to combat

DEFAMATION FACTORY

the "infection" of so-called anti-Semitism, both locally and globally.

It was to be under Foxman's purview that the worst public scandal in ADL's near-century of existence was about to break.

In 1993, shortly before Lyndon LaRouche was set to be released on parole, San Francisco native newspapers went abuzz with the news that the California police had conducted a raid of the Anti-Defamation League's San Francisco and Los Angeles offices. More shocking than the sudden joint raids themselves were the findings they yielded.

Reams upon reams of documentation obtained from over 600 different civic organizations and over 10,000 private citizens. Fruits of a long-running espionage campaign directed by The Anti-Defamation League of B'nai B'rith.

It was vintage ADL.

The police, upon a close inspection of the ADL-complied documentation, discerned that about 75% of those files had been obtained **illegally**. Some of the illegal documentation included classified private police files as well as personal DMV information, which, naturally, could not just be obtained from a quick phone-book or browser search.

What was peculiar about these files, other than the fact that they had been illegally obtained, was the fact that the majority of the organizations listed were liberal or left-leaning groups such as the

NAACP (National Association for the Advancement of Colored Peoples), La Raza, The National Indian Treaty Council, the San Francisco Labor Council, the Asian Law Caucus and a bevy of labor unions and Jewish groups who just so happened to be the wrong kind of Jew as far as Foxman and co. were concerned. Individuals targeted for monitoring included such influential leftist thinkers as linguist and Israel-critic, Noam Chomsky who was targeted specially due to his positive views on Palestinians (the ADL labeled him an "Arab apologist" in internal documentation) and also because of his criticism of old LaRouche adversary, Henry A. Kissinger.

The California spy ring had been largely the project of a one Roy Edward Bullock, known to his friends as "Cal," a barrel-chested weight-lifter from California and long-standing ADL operative who worked directly under the ADL's New York spy-king, Irwin Suall. A year prior to the scandal, Suall had stated that, in California, Roy Bullock was the ADL's "number 1 fact finder." *Fact finder*, to the ADL, appears to ever be a synonym for *spy*.

Yet, after the police seized the ADL's private and largely illegal information data-base, The League instantly distanced themselves from Bullock and with good reason.

One of the Arab-American groups which Bullock infiltrated was the ADC, or Arab-American Anti-Discrimination Committee of whom Alexander (Alex) Odeh was the local leader in the Orange County area. It also came out that Bullock had "befriended" Odeh for his trade. Police found both a key and floor-plan in Bullock's case files, the fruits of his surreptitious labor. The key belonged to Alex Odeh and the floor-plan described the ins and outs of the ADC office. Bullock was not linked to Odeh's murder but the very fact that he possessed such peculiar items doubtless raised many brows, as well it should. In addition to brows it should also have raised the question: Was Roy Bullock the individual who had planted the bomb which killed Alex Odeh? If so, why? He had, after all, both means and motive to commit the deed. The means, the key, the floor-plan and all the ancillary information he had collected concerning Odeh and his organization for the ADL. The motive is a little more murky but sufficient to say that the ADL and the ADC were on anything but friendly terms given the Palestinian-Israeli conflict.

The ADL directed, via internal memoranda, that their regional directors refer to "Cal" only as, "an individual who is alleged to have a relationship with the ADL." This, of course, was the opposite of the truth; in point of fact Bullock – who had always dreamed of being a spy – had worked with the ADL for over 40 years, ferrying information back and forth and sometimes operating in tandem with other intelligence agencies, foreign and domestic. Mounting evidence of Bullock and the ADL's relationship eventually lead the organization to give up the ghost and admit the connection, albeit in the most slippery of ways, describing him merely as a "private contractor." How perfectly nebulous.

BULLOCK'S BLUNDER & LAROUCHE'S RETURN

Foxman's League further elaborated that the files he had collected were solely for his "personal usage." If one did not know any better, one might begin to think that Foxman thought the American public very, very stupid.

Surprisingly this cover story melted quicker than play-dough in a steel-plant and, with the law out for Bullock, the ADL swooped in to protect their asset by cooking up a legal defense team for the erstwhile 007-wannabe. ADL's keen interest in protecting Bullock likely stemmed from more than merely his considerable prowess as an undercover agent, for the few photographs publicly available of Bullock, with a couple of exceptions, all show him standing next to the stubby, crook-faced, gremlin-of-a-man, Abraham Foxman. Likely, it was a question of personal loyalty as much as material gain and the very keen desire to cover their invidious track. Things got even worse for the ADL and their spy when their espionage ring was linked to a local police officer, a one, Tom Gerard who had, himself, been leaking confidential police information concerning Arab-Americans to The League.

Cover for Bullock was badly needed, for on January 25-26, San Francisco police officer, Ron Roth and several of his associates, including the assistant D.A., John Dwyer, attorney, Bob Breakstone and police sergeant, Bob Hulsey met with the spy for a thorough interview. Roth has been the very same man who had initially issued the warrant and search of the ADL offices in Los Angeles in the joint LA/SanFran raids which had sparked off the whole adventure. The interview yielded some very interesting information, chief among which was Bullock's personal connection to the roguish and charming police officer, Tom Gerard. Bullock noted that he had met Gerard in 1986 at the local ADL offices, had gotten to talking and, after the meeting, had gone to a McDonald's (which Bullock amusingly described as "that fine Scottish restaurant"). According to Bullock, Gerard had come to the ADL for assistance in freeing an Irish mercenary. The Irish mercenary was a friend of Gerard's who had run guns with a four-man crew to some "tin-pot dictator" to "some African country." Gerard, who was not a member of the group himself, relayed that these gun-running soldiers of fortune had been imprisoned in Brazil, en-route to whatever mysterious nation on the dark continent they had been heading to; Gerard wanted the ADL's help to get them released. Bullock said he'd talk to his handler, Irwin Suall, but told the officer not to get his hopes up. Despite the fact that nothing came of the mercenary situation, Gerard and Bullock fell into a fairly close working relationship, with both parties ringing up the other when they needed to uncover some pertinent piece of information. Bullock got insider police information and Gerard, access to the ADL's considerable master-spy index. The arrangement was a cozy and productive one, seemingly for all parties involved, Gerard and Bullock shored up any lack of information on their respective ends by inter-communication and the ADL continued to increase its massive and largely illegal database on

Arab-American civil rights activists, "pinkos," skinheads and Asian Law Caucuses. It also came out that Gerard had been doing some spying of his own, primarily upon Californian Arab and anti-apartheid groups. ADL's concern with African anti-apartheid activists is worth some consideration due their intensely pro-Israel policies. For instance, Abraham Foxman wrote a column in the *Huffington Post* in 2012 wherein he whole-heartedly agreed with the famous Israeli writer and political figure, Nathan (Natan) Sharansky, who emphatically stated that, "*it's anti-Semitism when Israel is demonized, when Israel is delegitimized and when a double-standard is used to assess Israeli behavior.*" This is an exceedingly poor argument on a number of levels, the first and foremost that if "anti-Semitism" is defined as a prejudicial hatred for the Jewish people then criticism of the state of Israel, in whatever fashion, can only ever be anti-Semitism if Israel represented ALL Jewish people, which it manifestly does not. Certainly it isn't good to "demonize" anyone, most would agree on this but what about when Israel is "delegitimized?" Of a certainty there are many people who do not think Israel as a state is legitimate, many of whom are American-Jews, does that make them "anti-Semitic?" No. That's foolishness and, ironically, the very kind of hapless demonization that Sharansky warned about, only coming from a different direction. The reasoning here is very poor, but given Foxman's intense, one might dare say fanatical, pro-Zionism, it is understandable though still highly suspect.

DEFAMATION FACTORY

After Bullock's initial police interview things began to heat up rather quickly. So much so that after Tom Gerard was questioned by the FBI on suspicion of illegal spying, he fled to the Philippines! Clearly he had not read Macbeth. Gerard left behind a panoply of suspicious material including passports, personal papers and driver's licenses in over 10 different countries. Now why on earth would a police officer have that many passports? Why was he constantly globetrotting when he should have been attending to his duties to protect the American public? More shocking than the documents of personal identification were the black hood and the photographs of men, chained-up and blind-folded which Gerard left behind. Assuredly, the victims of Gerard's unorthodox interrogation techniques in pursuit of some badly needed information required for his illicit trade. In addition to all of this grotesque paraphernalia, Gerard also possessed extensive information concerning, of all things, Central American death squads. When Gerard returned to the States to be reunited with his family he was seized by police at the San Francisco International Airport and charged with 11 felonies, including theft of confidential government documents (yet little was made about the black hood or the death squads or the tied up men!). Upon his return Gerard claimed to have been working for the CIA (Central Intelligence Agency and further stated that he had returned from the Philippines because he believed the CIA had put out a contract on his life! The CIA refused to comment on the incident, neither confirming nor denying Gerard's statements.

Gerard eventually pleaded "no contest" to the charge of unauthorized use of a police computer and was given a slap on the wrist; a dainty sentence of 3 years' probation, 45 days in jail and a $2,500 fine.

Bullock, realizing the danger inherent in being connected to the criminal, quickly threw his former "friend" under the bus, stating that Gerard had been illegally selling information but that he had nothing to do with it. Bullock, who was quite well known in San Francisco's burgeoning homosexual scene, added, "I may be gay, but I'm a straight arrow."

In a public interview which took place after Gerard's flight, Bullock admitted that he had indeed infiltrated various different right-wing organizations for the ADL. This information was widely circulated all around the California area.

Suspicion of Bullock and the ADL were growing, despite their protestations.

Yet, Bullock maintained that his activities (and those of the ADL's) were above-board, that the only mistake he had, perhaps, made was in selling his illegally obtained information to the South African apartheid government. Nothing to see here folks, move on! Not only did Bullock state that he wasn't in the wrong, he also cried foul, stating in a press interview in 1993 that, "This case [the ADL spy investigation] has been more a campaign of vilification," he continued rather melodramatically. "Why are they doing it? Why? Why? Why?"

Due to the mounting evidence and suspicion surrounding Bullock and the ADL, San Francisco District Attorney, Arlo Smith opened up his own investigation into the affair to determine conclusively whether or not the rights of private citizens had been violated.

Arlo's investigation was extensive and thorough and very shortly he produced a 700-page manuscript documenting what he alleged was a nationally syndicated spy-ring overseen and engineered by the Anti-Defamation League itself. Yet Smith was between a rock and a hard place, for if he attempted to prosecute the ADL he would instantly lose the trust and support of the influential Jewish community who would stick-up for the ADL, either because they bought into the lie that The League was a virtuous "civil rights organization" or simply due to a potent ethno-tribal bias, or, indeed, some combination of the two. Smith desperately wanted to be the California State Attorney General and it was in large part due to the local Jewish community that he was elected to D.A. Therefore, Smith pulled the case, essentially letting the ADL off the hook for prospective political gain.

On November 15th, 1993, Arlo Smith released a statement pertaining to why he had ceased litigation. The article in question read:

> *"The SFDA and Defendants agree that litigation concerning Defendant's activities would involve disputed issues of fact and law and that such litigation would be expensive and time-consuming both to the SFDA and Defendants."*

It should go without saying that such litigation ALWAYS deals with "disputed issues of fact and law," which DA Smith doubtless well enough knew.

What Smith seemed not to know, however, was that his fears had already manifested as soon as he opened the case. Simply looking into the ADL had incurred the scorn of California's politically powerful and peculiarly vengeful, Jewish community, who turned upon the hapless District Attorney like ants upon a wounded spider.

Though the ADL was "off the hook" they weren't entirely in the clear. The ADL might have escaped litigation but they had their public image to consider. To this end the ADL solemnly promised that it would not obtain nor solicit any non-public information from government officials. The League announced that instead of getting their information from crooked cops and underhanded gay weightlifters, they would now create a "Hate Crimes Reward Fund" which would function as a contract-hub for those who had committed "hate crimes," and would provide financial compensation for any information which lead to the arrest of said individuals. The fact that this so-called, Hate Crimes Reward Fund, effectively provides powerful incentives for people to find "hate crimes" where they do not exist, is notable.

Despite the overwhelming evidence that the ADL had indeed been the architect of an enormous espionage operation which spied on innocent members of the American public, invading their privacy and often stealing their information, no real justice was ever done. The ADL would escape largely unharmed with their greater public reputation intact and their coffers only slightly hindered. The most they would have to cough up was a few thousand dollars to cover the court costs of a few particularly vengeful victims of their illicit trade who were, themselves, eventually fatigued out of litigation.

The ADL had been caught red-handed in criminal activity and merely shrugged; Abraham "The Fox" Foxman was doubtless pleased.

As the 90s dragged on, the ADL increasingly turned their petulant antennae towards the newest horizon of "hate" in need of some good, old-fashioned censorship, the information-superhighway known as The Internet.

Chapter VII

"HATE" GOES VIRAL:
THE ADL IN THE DIGITAL AGE
(1990s-present)

"We are in a major transformation because our critical infrastructures, economy, personal lives, and even basic understanding of – and interaction with – the world are becoming more intertwined with digital technologies and the Internet. In some cases, the world is applying digital technologies faster than our ability to understand the security implications and mitigate potential risks. State and nonstate actors increasingly exploit the Internet to achieve strategic objectives, while many governments – shaken by the role the Internet has played in political instability and regime change – seek to increase their control over content in cyberspace. The growing use of cyber capabilities to achieve strategic goals is also outpacing the development of a shared understanding of norms of behavior, increasing the chances for miscalculations and misunderstandings that could lead to unintended escalation. Compounding these developments are uncertainty and doubt as we face new and unpredictable cyber threats. In response to the trends and events that happen in cyberspace, the choices we and other actors make in coming years will shape cyberspace for decades to come, with

DEFAMATION FACTORY

potentially profound implications for US economic and national security. In the United States, we define cyber threats in terms of cyber attacks and cyber espionage. A cyber attack is a non-kinetic offensive operation intended to create physical effects or to manipulate, disrupt, or delete data. It might range from a denial-of-service operation that temporarily prevents access to a website, to an attack on a power turbine that causes physical damage and an outage lasting for days. Cyber espionage refers to intrusions into networks to access sensitive diplomatic, military, or economic information."

James Clapper, *Worldwide Threat Assessment of the US Intelligence Community* (2013)

With the formation of the Internet proper the world was more interconnected than ever. Information flowed freely – too freely for the ADL's idiosyncratically draconian tastes.

In 1985, the ADL published a 15-page document entitled, *Computerized Networks of Hate*, and was one of the group's first forays into combating what they termed in their internal and public documentation as "high technology" radicalization.

In 1996 the ADL put out a publication called *The Web of Hate: Extremists Exploit the Internet*. The 61-page document was a more in-depth and updated version of *Computerized Networks of Hate* and explored both the nature of the still congealing Internet as well as various different dissident political and philosophical organizations thereupon, all of which The League had labeled as "haters." Some of these included obvious targets such as the KKK,

Don Black and his white nationalist Internet forum, Stormfront, David Duke, The National Alliance, Tom Metzger's W.A.R. (White Aryan Resistance) and various dissident scholars, such as Eustace Mullins. The ADL, at this period in time, took particular pains to single out Mullins who they slapped with the rather colorful label of, "hoary anti-Semite". Mullins was a singularly astute individual and, regardless of his controversial positions, he was an extremely thorough researcher (so much so that he worked for a time as a researcher for the Library of Congress), despite this the ADL skipped over his research and his arguments themselves, preferring instead to hit him over and over again with slur after slur.

Here, it is pertinent to pause and examine the tactic here deployed against Mr. Mullins for it is one which The League are ever ready to use, at every turn, against anyone they deem sufficiently ideologically deviant. That being: hater or hate-monger. One of the problems with the ADL's perennial tactic of labeling all of their targets as "haters" is that it reduces the organizations and individuals which are being referenced down to a single unitary factor in the eye of the public given the obscure nature of most of the organizations which The League rabidly engages in smear-campaigning. For example, as well known as Mullins was at the time, he was not sufficiently equipped, either financially or socially, to effectively combat the full force of the massive, international defamation machine which the ADL had become. Furthermore, and indeed, rather ironically, reducing all opponents to nothing other than malignant, spittle-dripping hate-mongers ends up having the precise opposite effect than was intended. The more a group like the SPLC or ADL derides largely powerless individuals or groups who express dissident thought, the more those already marginalized groups move further and further off into the proverbial "fringe." When you have a young man, confused, angry and seeking answers, direction and purpose, who, due his rootlessness and angst, becomes disenchanted with society at large such individuals will often take refuge, rightly or wrongly, in obscure, rigid and dissident ideologies. These ideologies then move the disenchanted and isolated individual further from the mainstream (again, rightly or wrongly) and then along comes ADL saying, "We disagree with you, therefore, you're a horrible person!" Ask yourself how you would respond if placed in such a situation. With anger and resentment and occasional fantasies of revenge of course, that is only natural.

Returning our attention back to ADL's *Web of Hate* booklet one will instantly recognize the disturbing fact that what is described or hinted at being truly American is simply that which the ADL dictates. That is to say, the booklet essentially serves, in a rather subtle way, as a sort of manifesto of what the ADL imagines America to be. The problem here is that, as a matter of historical fact, America is not, nor has ever been as they imagine it (obsessively multicultural, Judeo-centric, "color-blind," totally gender-egalitarian, etc.) and in some places, declare it to be. This is not to make a value judgment on American culture, to say whether it should or shouldn't be thus, or the ADL's ideal conception thereof, but merely to say it is always a horrible idea to blame figures of a country's past (and those shaped by them) for not instantly re-configuring to one's idealized image thereof. Something else that should be noted about the booklet is that it largely goes after rather low-hanging fruit, skin-heads, strange and tiny neo-Nazi groups, etc. Almost no academics are contained within and when they are, as with Mullins, the ADL doesn't take them to task on their arguments but rather simply brushes them, highhandedly, aside with the usual laundry list of epithets.

"Hater," "bigot," "anti-Semite," and so on and so on.

But then again, to be fair, the ADL never claimed to care about sound argumentation.

In 1998, two years after the publication of *Web of Hate*, the ADL created a program known as the "Hate Filter." The so-called Hate Filter was a software program that, as its name suggests, was completely dedicated to blocking out any websites which produced or offered content which denigrated what the group termed "immutable characteristics" of a person or group. The ADL defined these characteristics as being primarily three-fold, race, sexual orientation and religion. Now, rather obviously, one can not in any wise change their race, their very genetic composition, so this seems a reasonable thing to get agitated over were some website to be in the business of doing nothing but, say, defaming Anglo-Saxons for being Anglo-Saxons and without stating what it was fundamentally about Anglo-Saxons as a group that was so objectionable. Yet the remaining two characteristics on the ADL's list are far from "immutable." For instance, religion is by no means unchangeable. It might indeed be a very difficult thing for a man who was baptized into the Catholic Church at birth to convert to mainline Protestantism, but it is something which is by no means impossible, especially given that this happens with some regularity all across the world. There is a bevy of websites which are, in fact, dedicated to nothing but religious conversion stories and individuals who have made a career over their conversion from irreligion to religion (such as the atheist-critical, Christian, David Wood) or vice-versa (such as the Christian-critical, atheist TV personality, Matt Dillahunty) or from one religion to another, etc. Sufficient doubt in the tenets of any given faith doctrine over a long period of time, combined with acute and extended social pressures, are often more than enough to sway an individual from any given religion, no matter how rigorous its creed or ancient its tradition. The stance on the issue of sexual orientation is slightly more complicated but no less mistaken. For whilst it is largely true that a heterosexual man cannot change the fact that he is attracted to women (least, certainly not on a whim), he most certainly can change whether or not he acts upon said attraction and to what degree.

Unfortunately, such nuanced distinctions can hardly be expected to stop the ADL once they've sunk their fangs into the raw, yielding flesh of a new and promising censorship campaign and with the information superhighway open to them, the campaign would be a big one.

The ADL Hate Filter, an integral part of The League's now burgeoning Internet presence, was created in conjunction with The Learning Company, an American tech conglomerate specializing in educational software. The Learning Company had previously created a software program which they termed CyberPatrol, an Internet filter designed for public consumption. The CyberPatrol program was widely utilized across various public domains, including schools, libraries and businesses to block out sites which were considered "NSFW," that is to say, "Not safe for work." The HateFilter program, an add-on to CyberPatrol, was to be the vanguard for what ADL's national chairman, Howard Berkowitz, would describe as "a full-blown battle against high-tech hate." One would think it reasonable to assume that "hatred" real or imagined, when encountered online, would be considerably less of a hassle as there is no immediate threat of violence nor the same kind of psychosomatic pressures at play in a volatile face-to-face confrontation. For example, if someone tells you that they are "going to kill you" via an online chat program you will likely furrow your brows in surprise or disgust and then respond in either a reprimanding or scathing or post-ironic manner. If someone tells you they are "going to kill you" to your face, you will much more likely head for the hills or strike them first in self-defense (if you find their tone credibly threatening). The difference cannot be overstated. However, The League vehemently disagreed and to this day disagrees with that simple but resoundingly accurate delineation.

In an ADL published paper melodramatically entitled, *COMBATING EXTREMISM IN CYBERSPACE: THE LEGAL ISSUES AFFECTING INTERNET HATE SPEECH* (2000), the organization stated that [italicization mine]:

> "The Internet generation, unfortunately, is seriously at *risk of infection* by this *virus of hate*. Not only is this *virus* present on the Internet today; it is being spread around the globe, in the wink of an eye – or, more accurately, with the click of a mouse. This exciting new medium allows extremists easier access than they have ever had before to a potential audience of millions, a high percentage of whom are young and gullible. It also allows haters to find and communicate cheaply and easily with like-minded bigots across borders and oceans, to promote and recruit for their cause while preserving their anonymity, and even to share instructions for those seeking to act out their intolerance in violent ways.
> The spread of *this virus* poses one more important question. What is the most effective way to respond to this dark side of the Internet?"

Did you catch that? Hate is not merely a strong and primal emotion which occurs naturally in human beings, both for better and for worse – oh no – to the ADL, "hate" is described *as a virus*. Not figuratively but literally.

Now, I am no mind-reader but I am reasonably confident that the individual, or individuals, who penned that article (and many former and subsequent articles of a similar nature) do not literally believe that hate is some kind of mind virus that parasitizes an individual and leaps from host to host like the larval, face-grasping Xenomorphs of Ridley Scott's *Alien*. It is far more likely that many among the ADL's inner circle understand the ridiculous nature and often patently false quality of such assertions but continue to make and propagate them for some ideologically misbegotten notion of "the greater good," to help promulgate the ideal of, as they so very much love to say, "A world without hate."

Let us here pause for a moment to consider this tag-line: "A world without hate." It is, after all, a phrase which the ADL liked so much that they had it trademarked. "A world without hate" is also the catchphrase which adorns their website as well as their main Twitter page (at least as I write this in September of 2017) and can be seen almost invariably whenever and wherever the organization is involved with anything. So let us envision this "world without hate." Think about that a moment. I mean close your eyes and really picture it. A pedophile defiles your son and daughter; what is the response? Is the reasonable response forgiveness for the reprobate? Apathy? A shake of the head and wag of the finger? Mild irritation? Merely sadness at the crime which has been perpetrated? Or what of the man who declares that he despises you and all you stand for and will, because of this, see you ruined or dead? Is the appropriate and reasonable response here an admission of slight vexation?

No. Nor has it ever been. It has been hatred. Hatred for those who hate or grievously wrong an individual or group is not, regardless of what anyone might tell you, an unreasonable response. It may not always, it is certainly true, be the best response, but it is certainly not irrational nor any kind of "virus" of the mind. Generally speaking, humans do not hate things without some reason, explicit or implicit, whether one finds this justifying or not is another matter entirely, but that reason itself is important. If every spark of irritation, however minor and insignificant, incurred a response of wrathful loathing, then we might indeed wish to imagine the ADL's world without hatred. But this is simply and quite demonstrably not the case. All but the most aberrant personalities hate that which is counter to their selfsame well-being and the well-being of those for whom they care. This tends to hold true whether that thing which is counter to one's well-being is a real, or merely perceived, threat. To embrace murderous brigands who seek your destruction, or to merely treat them with indifference is patently suicidal (as the brigands will not be swayed by either eventuality), one's more primal side understands this and the reptile brain recoils in response to say – "Do not embrace that vile thing, destroy it or it will destroy you!" Yet the ADL would lead every sane and rational and upright-thinking person to believe that one's own biological drive to self-preservation, that is to say, hatred, is, in every conceivable instance, not only unjustified and unjustifiable, but *evil*. What is ironic is that this belief system itself is, if anything, the very definition of evil due to the fact that it necessitates its adherents believe that they alone are without hatred.

But here I do not wish to wax melodramatic – it is not at all my intention to paint all members of the ADL as inherently evil. That would be an absurd and unsustainable assertion. Indeed, many of the ADL's rank-and-file and, occasionally, members of its board, are exceedingly well-meaning individuals, such as Carl Pearlston.

Carl Pearlston was, for many years, a high-ranking member within The League, who had devoted himself totally to their project. Being himself a Jew, he was deeply concerned about both the heritage and traditions of his people and their future safeguarding from perceived socio-political threats. Due to these convictions, Mr. Pearlston looked upon the ADL of the 1970s as a stalwart defender of the Jewish people, an upright pillar that supported the broader Jewish-American community. He was so enamored with the group (he described his relationship with the ADL as a "love affair") that he decided to join and swiftly rose up through the ranks until he achieved the prestigious position of regional board member. He was then further promoted to the Executive Committee during the tumultuous years of the Civil Rights protests which consumed and utterly transformed the cultural-political landscape of America. He was a somewhat peculiar choice for the ADL given the fact that Mr. Pearlston was a conservative Republican (of the classical school) whilst the overwhelming majority of the ADL staff at the time were of a decidedly liberal or progressive stripe. The ADL had always declared itself to be a non-partisan organization that was solely concerned with civil rights. Yet this was manifestly not the case, indeed, Mr. Pearlston describes the tenor of the ADL's inner fold as less akin to a non-partisan civil rights group and more akin to (in Pearlston's own words) some "Democratic Party Club."

Pearlston's more conservative ideological leanings came to the fore in 1994 when an ADL operative by the name of David Cantor wrote a lengthy treatise on the order of The League detailing the nature of the so-called "religious right" in America. The piece was called, *The Religious Right: The Assault on Tolerance and Pluralism* and entailed a bevy of extremely harsh criticisms and allegations concerning numerous, primarily Christian, religious leaders such as Rev. Jerry Falwell, Pat Robertson and Jay Sekulow. The central thesis of the piece was that the "religious right" was, as the title so forthrightly puts it, assaulting American "tolerance and pluralism" via perverting scriptural doctrine to serve their own sinister interests. Very few Americans are particularly sanguine about the idea of religious totalitarianism and so naturally, were some individuals or groups to be advocating draconian theocracy push-back in the form of harsh criticism would be quite reasonable. However, the problem with Mr. Cantor's piece was that he made absolutely no effort whatsoever to contact any of the individuals or organizations whom he maintained were ruining the country. This information came straight from the horse's mouth, so to speak, as Cantor, in dialogue with the political paper, *The New York Times*, frankly admitted as much; he admitted straight out that he had not spoken to the individuals he had slandered! Nor did Mr. Cantor properly source the quotes he utilized for his lengthy treatise, rather he often employed quotes which he attributed to the religious leaders in his piece which *they had never said*, rather, the quotes were written by said religious leader's political opponents. Needless to say, this total breach of journalistic ethics inspired a firestorm of criticism against both Cantor and the ADL itself. A question also hung over the affair: Why would the ADL, one of the preeminent champions (at least ostensibly) of Judaism and the Jewish Community at large, wage all-out political and cultural war on right-leaning Christians who had, up until that point been the Jewish Communities greatest allies? The answer remains largely unclear but what was, however, quite clear was that not every member of the ADL was quite so sanguine with the slander campaign. Some detractors included such prominent members of The Anti-Defamation League as Phillip Aronoff, Fred Zeidman and Gary Pollard. Gary Pollard, a notable leader of one of the ADL's Houston chapters, was particularly put-out over the affair and later conducted an interview with *New York* magazine wherein he flatly stated that "the liberal Jewish community," was, "everything that's wrong with this country." Pat Robertson himself personally and very vocally protested the slander which the ADL had heaped on him. Surprisingly, this protest worked and the social blow-back was such that there was nothing for it but for then ADL leader, Abraham Foxman to write a letter of apology wherein he frankly admitted to the slanderous misinformation contained within Cantor's hit-piece. Foxman also withdrew an allegation that Robertson had stated that Jews were "spiritually deaf" and "blind." The Jewish JWR columnist Mona Charen wrote of the affair:

> "The ADL has committed defamation. There is no other conclusion to be reached after reading its new report, *The Religious Right: The Assault on Tolerance and Pluralism* in America. It is sad that an organization with a proud history of fairness should have descended to this kind of character assassination and name calling."

Another prominent member of the ADL who objected to the slander was none other than Carl Pearlston himself who joined his peers in decrying the peculiar attack on the subsection of America which had previously been the ADL's foremost champion.

It was far from the first time Pearlston would clash with his compatriots. The ADL took supreme exception to a particular radio broadcaster by the name of Laura Catherine Schlessinger who was primarily known from her radio program, *The Dr. Laura Program*. The ADL detested Schlessinger's (dour) views on homosexuals and were, at the time, considering speaking out against her. Pearlston would later personally recount that, in an intimate board meeting with top ADL brass, he objected quite strongly to the idea of bringing a critical social campaign against Ms. Schlessinger on the grounds that she was a Jew who was only espousing traditional Jewish views about sex, marriage and homosexuality. Should not, Pearlston argued, the ADL stand up for Ms. Schlessinger on these grounds rather than try and tear her down? Was it not the duty of the Anti-Defamation League to stand up for the Jewish folk and for the values that Jews had traditionally upheld even if one might disagree with them in a personal capacity? The ADL's overwhelming response was a resounding: "NO."

Somewhat later, Mr. Pearlston attended yet another ADL meeting concerning the issue of school vouchers. The ADL was vehemently opposed to the idea of school vouchers, this despite the fact that vouchers – that which gave parents the ability to choose what schools their children go to – was protected under the US constitution. The matter was going through the courts and shortly the Supreme Court would rule on the constitutionality of school vouchers to settle the matter. Pearlston queried to Abraham Foxman what the ADL would do if the court's ruled in favor of constitutional protection for vouchers. Foxman responded ominously, "You shouldn't have asked that question."

This here sounds more like the language of some mafioso than that of an ostensibly peaceful civil rights organization! If one knew nothing of Foxman, one might have next assumed to hear him say he'd make Pearlston a "pair of cement shoes" should he persist in his line of inquiry.

After this incident what Pearlston had long suspected about the upper echelons of the organization now came rushing to the fore of his mind; the ADL, he realized all at once, was effectively a clerisy wherein certain forms of knowledge and certain questions were considered so vile as to be beyond utterance, indeed, beyond even conception. Pearlston later wrote of the meeting with Foxman, "the bloom was really off the romance."

Days and weeks wore on after Pearlston's unpleasant run in with his pudgy, bespectacled superior and several more disconcerting threads of thought began emerging and weaving themselves together in his consciousness. The ADL had begun moving away from its initial mission statement of working to expose and fight defamation of Jews. Now it was actively fighting to expose and fight "hate" itself despite the fact that actual, tangible hatred of Jews was quite scarce in America (and most of the rest of The West) and getting only scarcer. Pearlston took issue with this due to the fact that "defamation" was a tangible action, it was something which one does to another whereas "hate" was just a state of mind that did not necessarily impinge upon anyone else any more than irritation or elation did. The ADL believed that by changing the mind of "the haters" they could effectively change their actions which was (and still is as of this writing) a vexed endeavor given the fact that when you try to prosecute people, either judicially or extra judicially for "hate crime" what you are essentially doing is criminalizing thought itself. Witch-hunting heretics.

Realizing at this point that the ADL shared more in common with Heinrich Kramer than a true-blue liberal civil rights group, Pearlston, with a heavy heart and more than a little consternation, tendered his resignation. He would go on to pen a paper entitled, *The ADL Pushes "Tolerance?" Why I'm leaving After 25 Years.* The paper goes into some detail about the inner workings of the ADL as well as why Pearlston left, chief among those reasons was the pardoning of elusive businessman and criminal-swindler, Marc Rich.

The Marc Rich saga began on September 19th, 1983 when Rich, a fabulously wealthy Jewish-American commodities trader, along with his partner, Pincus Green, were indicted by a Federal grand jury for 48 million dollars' worth of tax evasion. The case was immediately noteworthy due to the massive sum, which made it the single largest case of tax fraud in history up to that point. The charges were a staggering 51 counts of tax evasion, racketeering and fraud.

Both men, upon being asked to comment, declined offers for interviews but stated firmly that they were innocent of the charges.

What happened was that both had been selling oil which was under US price controls for free market prices. Rich and Green then took their ill-gotten gains and shifted them to oversea accounts and then falsified transaction invoices between Rich and one of Rich's Swedish trading firms called Marc Rich & Company A.G. These document falsifications generated 33 million in illicit tax deductions. This devious scheme was aided by Listo Petroleum Inc., a company whose vice president was a 38-year-old named Clyde Meltzer who was a close oil trading business acquaintance of Rich.

Just like Marc "King of Oil" Rich and Green, Meltzer, who at the time of the indictment, lived in Manhattan, could not be reached for comment.

Given the underhanded nature of the aforementioned individual's ventures and the evidence aligned against them, one would have thought they would be made to pay for their trickster ways and that would be an end to it. However, this was not to be the case, for Rich and co. had a very vocal and powerful ally. None other than the ADL itself.

The reason the ADL took up for the "King of Oil" and co. was due in large part to Abraham Foxman's personal relationship to President Bill Clinton, Marc Rich and his wife, Denise Rich.

Rich had been traveling in Switzerland during the time the charges of corruption were leveled against him and, insisting he was not guilty, decided it was wise not to return to the United States. Given the fact Rich faced 300 years in prison should he have returned to his country, it is understandable that he waxed hesitant. Due to his aloofness and, what, I think we can properly and accurately call cowardice, Rich became a wanted man.

The man's fugitive status was so great that Rich was even included on the FBI's top 10 most wanted list; he would remain on that list for many years. Nothing seemed able to move Rich from his foreign perch, not even the death of his daughter, and her subsequent funeral, in 1996, drew him back to the states.

On the 20th of January, 2001, President Bill Clinton, in his last day in office, bestowed a full presidential pardon upon Rich, clearing him of all charges. It was a highly controversial move, especially given the timing. Former President Jimmy Carter publicly stated that he strongly suspected the motivation for Clinton's magnanimity rested in Rich's massive financial contributions. In Carter's own words, "I don't think there is any doubt that some of the factors in his pardon were attributable to his large gifts. In my opinion, that was disgraceful." The specific donations to which President Carter was referring came from Rich's wife, Denise, who contributed 1 million US dollars to both Bill and Hillary Clinton, both of whom were heavily involved in politics at the time. $100,000 of Rich's funds went to Hillary Clinton's senate campaign. $450,000 of Rich's funds went to the Clinton Library. And so on and so on.

As the old American adage goes: Follow the money.

The money leads us to one of the foremost champions of Rich's pardon, none other than Abraham Foxman, leader of the ADL at the time. The reason? The bespectacled and perpetually smiling Foxman had received around $250,000 dollars from Rich himself. Foxman even went so far as to write letters to Clinton in an attempt to secure a pardon for Rich. Rabbi Irving Greenberg of the US Holocaust Memorial Council and Shlomo Ben-Ami, the then foreign aid minister to Israel, also agitated on Rich's behalf.

Such agitation appears to have worked for as we already covered, Clinton did indeed free Rich and would later go on to state that the primary reason he arranged a pardon for the oil shyster was due to "Jewish pressure." Clinton would also go on to say that, "Israel did influence me profoundly."

A couple of points likely jump out at the inquiring mind concerning the Foxman/Rich situation. First and foremost, Pearlston was proved correct; the ADL ostensibly stands in opposition to defamation, specifically of the Jewish people and yet that had absolutely nothing to do with the Rich case. Whilst it is true that Marc Rich was both Jewish and an active member of the world-wide Jewish community (he had many deep ties to Israel), it is not true that he was being defamed in any manner. He was manifestly guilty of the crimes of which he was accused; end of story. This realization should raise some eyebrows, especially given the hefty financial contributions Rich made to the ADL which make it very clear that Foxman only interceded for Rich because of, as we say in America, "the dough."

Foxman and the ADL, however, had their tentacles in many more fields of interest than just the Rich Case during that time. 2001 also saw the ADL continue its foray into Internet censorship, building off of their previous successes with such programs as the "HateFilter" browser. At the time the ADL had established hundreds of offices all across the USA, Europe and Israel and were playing with a $46-million-dollar budget. Even still the massive organization was nervous, no matter how big they got and no matter how many different walls of propaganda they erected, there were always information holes where their narrative was fractured or broken away by rogue elements, dissidents and truth-seekers. Rich was merely the most recent and scandalous of these "holes" that, to the perceptive onlooker, exposed a seedy underbelly of graft, defamation and ideological fanaticism.

The League's information stranglehold had, at this point, been totally reset with the Internet – too many ports from which too many "haters" could shout, unabated and unopposed.

Their hackles were raised.

The ADL's task of stamping out everything which they deemed "hateful" was further complicated by the fact that, as far as free speech matters

DEFAMATION FACTORY

on the Internet were concerned, the United States government was not, and is not, always the primary arbitrator; indeed, more often than not, such issues are actually decided by ISPs (Internet Service Providers) rather than any particular state apparatus. What this means is that all of the clout which the ADL had built up in Washington via lobby groups and their contacts in Israel was rendered almost completely meaningless by the rise of the Internet.

Despite all their booklets critiquing online "hate" groups and attempts to shut down websites they didn't like, ADL was swimming upstream. Their efforts in cyberspace were proving relatively ineffective. They required more infrastructure and influence. They needed more traffic-controllers on the information superhighway. Yet, before The League could acquire them, there was something of a snag.

The Armenian Genocide.

On August 17th of 2007, Andrew H. Tarsey, ADL Regional Director of New England, was fired from his post after voicing his concern over The Anti-Defamation League's refusal to acknowledge The Armenian Genocide *as* a genocide. The Armenian Genocide (also referred to as the Armenian Holocaust) occurred from 1914 to 1923 when the Ottoman Empire made a concerted effort to completely eradicate the Armenian People. Estimates of the total death toll from the event range from 800,000 to 1,800,000 Armenians killed (the most commonly accepted death-toll figure published by academics is 1.5 million). The Turkish government, at this time, vociferously denied that the term "genocide" was accurate and furthermore legally penalized their citizenry should they speak out against the state in such a fashion.

Turkey, at this time was the lone Muslim ally of Israel and with the ADL at this point basically operating as a propaganda arm for the Israeli government had a very strong source of motivation to clamp down on anyone making hay over the Armenian affair. Since the ADL bears a fierce loyalty to Israel and Turkey is its ally, Americans who speak out concerning the Armenian genocide were viewed as damaging to Israel's relationship with Turkey due to the close relationship between Israel and the USA. In other word's the ADL snuffed out Tarsey's career to protect perceived Israeli/Turkish stability.

The move outraged many, such as former ADL board member, Steve Grossman, who said of the Tarsey Affair, "My reaction is that this was a vindictive, intolerant, and destructive act, ironically by an organization and leader whose mission – fundamental mission – is to promote tolerance."

Tarsey himself stated that he had been internally conflicted over the issue of ADL silence and cover-up concerning the Armenian Genocide for weeks before he decided to speak up. He relayed his displeasure through a direct phone conversation with none other than National Director Abraham Foxman wherein Tarsey stated that he found the

ADL's position on the Armenian Genocide "morally indefensible." Tarsey's criticisms were intensified by a chorus of ADL detractors (many of whom were Jews themselves) who took particular umbrage to the fact that Foxman regularly referred to himself as a "holocaust survivor" and yet would not take up for those who objectively did survive attempted genocide. If Foxman realized the hypocrisy, he kept it to himself, however, he made his position on Mr. Tarsey very public, stating that, "We've taken a position," and that he hoped Tarsey would be open to "conversation." Tarsey was indeed amenable to conversation as he would later join back up with the ADL, only to quit once again and become even more critical of their efforts!

The firing affair, however, had consequences that stretched far beyond just Tarsey himself. For instance, just before his firing, Tarsey had spoken in the heavily Armenian-populated city of Watertown, Massachusetts. After he was fired, the Armenian community of Waterford banded together to voice their protest of the town's ADL funded anti-bigotry program called No Place for Hate, viewing the ADL's silence on their people's genocide as both a slight and a hypocritical lack of adherence to the organization's stated principals. Shortly thereafter, the program was removed entirely by the Town Council.

Watertown was not the only town to cut its ties with the ADL; other municipalities such as, Arlington, Belmont, Medford, Newburyport, Newton, Northhampton, Peabody and Somerville all broke with the No Place for Hate program because of the scandal and became fiercely critical of The League's tactics.

In 2007, under immense social pressure, Abraham Foxman issued a public apology on behalf of the ADL concerning their previous position on the Armenian Genocide. What was curious about this public statement was that Foxman apologized not to the Armenian people, but to Turkey for inconveniencing them!

In 2012, in the month of October, the popular video sharing Internet platform, YouTube, created a program called the Trusted Flagger program. The Trusted Flagger program's primary purpose was to recruit "trusted" users to flag down videos on the website which were in violation of YouTube's terms of service since, due to sheer volume of user-input, the company couldn't manage every single video via their available staff. Video content which violated YouTube's terms of service included such things as hardcore pornography, violence, animal abuse and "hate-speech." Thus, a "trusted flagger" would, upon seeing any of the previously described content in a video, flag it and report the video to YouTube staff who would remove it upon their discretion after reviewing the contents.

Video flagging was at this time available to all normal users of the website but "trusted flaggers" who were invited into the program would be granted enhanced video flagging capabilities not provided to other lay users, such as the ability to remove up to 20 videos at once. The flagging program and YouTube and its parent company, Google, came under heavy scrutiny for this policy from both site users and external commentators who worried that both the amorphous quality of "hate-speech" coupled with the sheer scale of video removal now granted to a select few would result in draconian content purges not necessarily in violation of the site's actual rules. This was especially troubling for user's who made their living primarily or entirely through ad-revenue on their videos as a mass flag campaign could quite literally cause them to go hungry or lose their house.

James Brokenshire, security and immigration minister for the UK, commented on the affair, stating that YouTube and Google were attempting to ramp up efforts to address Internet content that "may not be illegal but certainly is unsavory." That is to say, YouTube and Google were cracking down on content which was neither illegal nor in violation of their user-content guidelines. This realization was made doubly troubling to YouTube users when it came to light that approximately 90 percent of all content marked by "trusted flaggers" was either taken down or placed in a restricted viewing state. To make matters worse, rumors began stirring that various governmental sector groups and civic NGOs, both domestic and foreign, were utilizing this powerful new flagging tool to their advantage at the expense of truth-seeking dissidents.

Such rumors were justified, for YouTube and Google had a powerful ally in their crusade against "unsavory" content, none other than the ADL itself.

On the 11th of December, 2008, the ADL and YouTube formally announced their partnership which meant that The League had been influencing YouTube policy for three years before the creation of the Trusted Flagger program. It is difficult to find information on the specific inside baseball which led to the creation of the program but it is not unreasonable to deduce that the ADL had a strong part to play in the video sharing site's newest content purging efforts given their long history of censorship and information suppression.

Some readers may not find this issue to be particularly important, despite all those who could lose their livelihoods from the Flagger Program and attendant policies. Indeed, many did not find it all that noteworthy at the time. Thus, it is worth noting that YouTube is one of the single most heavily trafficked sites in the entire world. YouTube and other similar streaming and video-sharing websites have become so popular that they have begun to largely replace traditional televised programming as the go-to source for information, news, comedy, films, music and more. As of 12/28/17, YouTube was the second most heavily trafficked website (in terms of page-views and visitors) in the entire world according to Alexa.com, a popular website ranking domain. Thus, to put the situation most starkly, YouTube (owned by the monopoly company, Google) controls the lion's share of the web's video which means they have the same kind of power that the TV executive's had before the rise of the Internet proper, only increased by several prominent orders of magnitude.

The flagging campaigns, blacklisting, restriction-placing and other forms of Internet censorship would only increase as the ADL built-up its digital foothold.

★

In 2014 The League went through a major change-up when it was announced that Abraham Foxman would be stepping down as National Director. The man slatted to fill his shoes was the younger, sleeker, 43-year-old Jonathan Greenblatt, a Jewish-American social entrepreneur and the CEO of the bottled water company, Ethos and business affiliate of coffee mega-corp, Starbucks. Greenblatt had also previously served as a special assistant under the Obama Administration and also had experience working as the Director of the Impact Economy Initiative at the George Soros funded Aspen Institute. He had liberal-progressive qualifications coming out his ears, a perfect fit for the ADL. During this same year the ADL, working in close conjunction with the website hosting company GoDaddy, had already removed 30 websites from the Internet which they considered to be, in part or totality, "anti-Semitic."

On July 2015, a 74-year-old Foxman relinquished the ADL directorship to Greenblatt. The

28-year reign of The Fox had come to an end but Greenblatt's regime was only just beginning.

★

Jonathan Greenblatt was, ostensibly, a more moderate and likable figurehead for the embattled ADL. Whereas Foxman was loud, braggadocios, curt and confrontational, Greenblatt was demure, soft-spoken, articulate and candid. One with no knowledge of the organization's history, methods and aims nor of Greenblatt's beliefs might indeed have been led to believe that Greenblatt was someone who would move The League in a bold new direction. A more positive and constructive direction.

Yet if you believed this you'd be sorry mistaken.

While Foxman came to be known as a rigid ideologue, demure Greenblatt would come to show that he was profoundly more dogmatic and zealous than Foxman could ever hope to be, and far more subtle as well.

November 13, 2016, Jonathan Greenblatt took to the social media platform Twitter to write, "We at @ADL_National oppose the appt (appointment) of Steve Bannon to sr (senior) role at @WhiteHouse bc (because) he & his alt-right are so hostile to core American values."

This message was accompanied by a screen-shot of an official ADL statement crafted by Greenblatt which stated:

> *"The Anti-Defamation League (ADL) commends President-elect Trump for appointing Reince Priebus White House Chief of Staff. Priebus has had a long career in politics and public life, and we wish him well in his new role.*
>
> *At the same time, the ADL strongly opposes the appointment of Steve Bannon as senior advisor and chief strategist in the White House. It is a sad day when a man who presided over the premier website of the 'alt-right' – a loose-knit group of white nationalists and unabashed anti-Semites and racists – is slated to be a senior staff member in the 'people's house.' We call on President-elect Trump to appoint and nominate Americans committed to the well-being of all of our country's people and who exemplify the values of pluralism and tolerance that make our country great."* – Jonathan Greenblatt, CEO, ADL.

The criticism was widely interpreted as a proxy accusation of anti-Semitism and racism. However, an article published the same day (Nov. 13, 2016) from the *Huffington Post* entitled, ***A White Nationalist Is the New White House Chief Strategist***, as well as a bevy of subsequent, similar offerings from various other, primarily left-wing, media outlets, left no mind in doubt about the liberal-establishment opinion of Bannon or what his appointment portended for the incoming Presidential Administration.

Yet, contrary to these allegations, Bannon had many firm friends in America's Jewish community, not least among them, Rabbi Shmuley Boteach, an accomplished orator, who wrote an open letter in *The Hill* to ADL CEO Jonathan Greenblatt. The letter read:

> *You recently attacked Bannon's appointment as senior adviser to the president, saying, "It is a sad day when a man who presided over the premier website of the 'alt-right' – a loose-knit group of white nationalists and unabashed anti-Semites and racists – is slated to be a senior staff member in the 'people's house.'" Your comment was widely – though perhaps unfairly – interpreted as accusing Bannon of anti-Semitism.*
>
> *I barely know Mr. Bannon, having met him for the first time last week at The New York Hilton. But I do know Joel Pollak, an orthodox Jew who is my friend of many years and is a senior editor at Breitbart. Joel is one of the proudest Jews I know and one of the premier fighters for Israel in the national media. He [Pollak] tells me that Steve Bannon has shown him, and the many other Jewish employees at Breitbart, especially those who are observant, incredible sensitivity and flexibility in helping them always keep the Sabbath and observe the Jewish holidays.*

In addition, Breitbart *has served as one of the leading publications in the United States that strongly opposed the Iran nuclear agreement, with its $150 billion given to the murderous Mullahs and their genocidal promise to perpetrate a second holocaust of the Jewish people.*

Mr. Pollak whom the rabbi mentions in his open letter also took the public stage to defend Steve Bannon's appointment, stating in an interview with CNN's Don Lemon that Mr. Bannon was not an anti-Semite and that, if anything he was "overly sensitive" to disparaging remarks made against Jews and often took offense on their behalf. Mr. Pollak also penned a piece at *Breitbart* entitled, *Stephen K. Bannon: Friend of the Jewish People, Defender of Israel*, wherein Pollak writes, "I have worked with Stephen K. Bannon, President-elect Donald Trump's new chief strategist and senior counselor, for nearly six years at *Breitbart News*. I can say, without hesitation, that Steve is a friend of the Jewish people and a defender of Israel, as well as being a passionate American patriot and a great leader."

Former *Breitbart* writer turned Bannon-critic, Editor-in-Chief of conservative media outlet, *DailyWire*, Ben Shapiro, himself a Jew, took to the web to state that the accusations against Bannon were highly overblown. In a column-piece entitled *3 Thoughts On Steve Bannon as White House 'Chief Strategist,'* Shapiro wrote, "I have no evidence that Bannon's a racist or that he's an anti-Semite; the

Huffington Post's blaring headline, 'WHITE NATIONALIST IN THE WHITE HOUSE,' is overstated." It is worth reiterating that Shapiro had absolutely no incentive to stick up for Bannon and goes on to bash the man in intensely hyperbolic fashion which makes Shapiro's claims seem all the more likely to be true.

So then, looking at this overall, three Jews, Shapiro, Boteach and Pollack, speak well of Bannon contrary to Greenblatt's official statement, revealing the insinuations of the ADL have been false. The fact that these opinions come from all possible angles of social relationship to Bannon – friend (Pollak), foe (Shapiro) and neutral party (Boteach) – and that they all agree on certain essential points of the man's character and behavior lends considerable credibility. So it would appear that the ADL was once again attempting to smear an individual who stood at political odds with them. Another instance of the defamation factory in full swing.

Shortly after their first article concerning Bannon, the ADL put out another article (the creation of which, I suspect, was a product of pressure from Bannon's considerable horde of defenders). The new ADL outing sounded like a *BuzzFeed* article, Stephen Bannon: *5 Things You Need to Know*. Number 5 of the "5 Things You Need to Know" was titled: 5. We Are Not Aware of Any Anti-Semitic Statements from Bannon.

It would seem that, for the moment, the ADL had met with defeat. They could not get the slander to stick to Bannon, but that did not mean they would stop trying to defame both Bannon, Trump, his entire administration and their entire support bloc which made up nearly half of the entire American public.

On November 17, 2016, at the New York based Never Is Now conference hosted by ADL, director Jonathan Greenblatt stated the following:

> "This was an election where a presidential candidate criticized Israel in a manner that evoked a blood libel; where another unapologetically tweeted a sinister Star of David meme that had been created by white supremacists; it promoted a campaign slogan that evoked the phrase most associated with notorious Nazi sympathizer Charles Lindbergh, and sponsored a closing television ad that echoed anti-Semitic conspiracies that have been used to justify anti-Jewish persecution for centuries. During this political season, we saw white supremacists use a triple parenthesis to target Jews online and simultaneously, relentlessly harass and intimidate Jewish journalists on social media with anti-Semitic tropes and horrific images of the Holocaust. In short, the American Jewish community has not seen this level of anti-Semitism in mainstream political and public discourse since the 1930s."

THE ADL IN THE DIGITAL AGE

Naturally, Greenblatt and the ADL at large received an extensive amount of criticism for these largely overblown statements given that some of the things mentioned, such as the "sinister Star of David" were pure fabrications as the star which is referenced was simply a star preset which is often employed in graphic design programs all across the globe. Specific attention was drawn to the director's comparison of modern-day America to National Socialist Germany. Greenblatt would go on to lay the blame for this perceived rise of "anti-semitism" almost exclusively at the feet of Donald J. Trump, the newly elected President of the United States of America.

At 4:48 AM, January 11th, 2017, President Donald Trump took to the social media and mini-blogging website, Twitter to complain about allegations that Russia had obtained compromising information on his person which had been leaked from government intelligence agencies.

He wrote, "Intelligence agencies should never have allowed their fake news to 'leak' into the public. One last shot at me. Are we living in Nazi Germany?"

The mainstream media went ballistic with the story. Yet, despite all the media furor the group which seemed to take the most umbrage at this innocuous off-hand remark was the ADL who instantly called upon the President to recant his statements. The League was so incited by the "tweet" that CEO Jonathan Greenblatt released a public statement. Greenblatt's press release read:

"The President-elect's use of Nazi Germany to make a political analogy is not only an inappropriate comparison on the merits, but it also coarsens our discourse and diminishes the horror of the Holocaust.

There are legitimate questions on all sides regarding foreign influence in the 2016 presidential race. But the United States has democratic elections, a free press, rule of law and a civil service – including our intelligence agencies – that is deeply loyal to the U.S. Constitution. These facts invalidate any analogies between America and totalitarian societies.

ADL always has maintained that glib comparisons to Nazi Germany are offensive and a trivialization of the Holocaust. We have a long record of speaking out when both Democrats and Republicans engage in such overheated rhetoric. It would be helpful for the President-elect to explain his intentions or apologize for the remark."

Despite all the hullabaloo over such a throwaway line, what is remarkable about this statement is that it is a totally hypocritical thing for Greenblatt to say as he had just recently done the very same thing. Recall his previous statement as pertains to the climate of the USA, "In short, the American Jewish community has not seen this level of anti-Semitism in mainstream political and public discourse since the 1930s."

THE ADL IN THE DIGITAL AGE

Greenblatt's speeches, even before taking over the ADL, are replete with similar statements comparing the United States of America to National Socialist Germany.

What this obvious double-standard reveals is that the ADL believes that it alone is entitled to make comparisons to National Socialist Germany, but should anyone else make similar comparisons, they are "cheapening the Holocaust," or are found to be, somehow, "anti-Semitic." To top it all off, this is coming from an organization which has actively worked to cheapen a different "holocaust," that being, The Armenian Genocide.

June 18, 2017, Google, via its official European blog, blog.google, announced plans for a new program which would crackdown on online "extremist" content on all their platforms but primarily upon YouTube. The article which announced this policy change to the platform was titled, *Four Steps We're Taking Today to Fight Terrorism Online*; the article noted that Google was working feverishly with government law-enforcement agencies and expert counter-extremism groups (i.e. the ADL) to institute their policies. The first step they announced was an increase in technological dedication to "identity extremist and terrorism-related videos." To fulfill such a commitment Google announced that they would be deploying more engineers to YouTube and their other platforms (such as G+) to create machine-learning programs whose purpose would be to identify and remove or restrict specific blacklisted content. The second step was to be a mass expansion of the Trusted Flagger YouTube program in addition to adding to their roster of "experts" 50 NGOs (Non-governmental organizations) to the 63 organizations with which Google was already working. All groups involved will have credentials pertaining to such issues as "hate-speech," "self-harm" and "terrorism." Thirdly – and most interestingly – the company vowed to take a "tougher stance on videos that clearly violate our policies." What this means is that one's videos can be censored from YouTube even if they are not in violation of any YouTube/Google policies. This then begs the natural question of why would Google and YouTube even both create site policies at all if they are meaningless guidelines? Why not just be honest and say what their "third step" actually entails; that is: "We may kick you off our site for good reasons, bad reasons or no reasons at all." Naturally, if Google were so forthright as this they would doubtless see a sudden drop in traffic and likely a quick ensuing boycott. Fourthly and lastly, Google promised to expand and dedicate more resources to counter radicalization efforts such as their Creators for Change program which works to end "hate and radicalization." To accomplish these goals, the article stated that Google would be working in tandem with a wide variety of other Internet mega-corporations such as Twitter, Facebook and

Microsoft in the hopes of fostering an international "anti-hate" forum.

At this point in time the ADL was one of the select contributing organizations listed on YouTube's Trusted Flagger program.

Surprise, surprise...

On the 11th of August 2017, the nation erupted into a frenzy as various right-wing political factions coalesced and marched upon Charlottesville, Virginia. From the 11th to the 12th of August, disaffected libertarians, constitutional and militia movement members, identitarian activists and white nationalists marched about waving flags and torches in and around Emancipation Park (formerly Lee Park) for an event titled the Unite the Right Rally. The rally was staged in protest of the planned take-down of the historical monument of Confederate Commander, Robert E. Lee and his trusted steed, Traveller. Lee was the historical figure from which the park derived its original name and was a man who had played a central role in the American Civil War; because of this he is highly venerated by many southerners even to this day. Many Americans, northerners and southerners, viewed the increasing pressure from social justice groups (such as BLM) to remove all confederate memorials across the country as a direct assault upon American heritage and identity, specifically, White American identity. This reaction was especially prominent among conservatives, paleoconservatives, right-leaning libertarians, neo-reactionaries and white nationalists and separatists. The Unite the Right Rally was organized by the controversial political activist Jason Kessler in response to a March 2016 statement given by the equally controversial Charlottesville vice-mayor, Wes Bellamy who called for the removal of the Lee statue on the basis that it represented "racial inequity."

This justification struck many Americans as odd; for if one took Mr. Bellamy's view as correct – that a statue of a historical figure who lived in more racially segmented times was inherently bad for the country – it logically follows then that what one must next do is take down ALL confederate statues, and then all Union statues as well. In effect, the process of historical revisionism, under the guidance of men like Bellamy, would never end because practically every statue in the United States of America pre-1960 was designed by, and patterned after, some figure who lived in a time in which the conception of race was markedly different. Many worried that the Bellamy justification (which was gaining ground all across the country from various liberal groups) would not end until the whole history of America had either been erased or re-written.

Various other event organizers gave responses similar to Jason Kessler's concerning the purpose of the rally. Nearly all agreed that their cultural heritage was under assault.

The colorful display turned decidedly deadly, however, when a young man named James A.

Fields drove his car into a crowd of radical protesters after his vehicle was struck by a bat being wielded by an unidentified agitator. During the collision a middle-aged woman by the name of Heather Heyer had a heart attack due to the shock of the event and died. A helicopter also crashed, some distance away from the event, killing two state troopers who were aboard.

A media firestorm quickly ensued, the whole of the mainstream media, left and right, banded together to "disavow" the participants of the rally as across the board "white supremacists," or, if they were feeling particularly generous, "white supremacist sympathizers." James A. Fields was instantly branded as a murderer and terrorist who had purposefully and maliciously run-over Heather Heyer and slain her, this despite the fact that she had died from shock rather than from blunt-force trauma. Some even blamed the rally participants for the helicopter crash, despite the fact that the vehicle likely crashed due to an unforeseen mechanical failure given that the aircraft had not collided whilst in mid-flight. Additionally, the crash had absolutely nothing to do with either the largely right-wing protesters or the largely left-wing counter-protesters.

A state of emergency was swiftly called by Virginia Governor, Terry McAuliffe and police moved in as violent ANTIFA agitators clashed with the Unite the Right coalition in Lee Park and beyond. The chaos spilling out into the city streets. Despite the fact that the police were called in to stop the violence and clear the area they stood down when the violence reached its zenith. Various live-streams from within the riot-zones showed numerous instances of heavily armed and armored police officers standing by as anarchists, liberal agitators and communist ANTIFA apparatchiks surged at the lawfully assembled rally participants, striking them and shouting vulgarities. One young black man was photographed attacking the Unite the Righters with a makeshift flamethrower.

Yet, despite how obviously in the wrong the counter-protesters were, the media establishment and NGO watch dogs moved in totality against the lawfully assembled.

On August 15th, 2017, Jonathan Greenblatt appeared on MSNBC News, streaming live from Tel Aviv, Israel, to discuss "right-wing extremism" which the ADL CEO contested was on the rise in America.

His opening remarks were in response to one of the MSNBC newscasters who asked Greenblatt to describe the "true threat" to America to which Greenblatt responded, "you mentioned a number of them, Neo-Nazis, the so-called alt-right, anti-government groups, neo-confederates; let's be clear, they're all part of the same white supremacist movement that is opposed to American values. There is no patriotism in white nationalism."

As Greenblatt spoke, various sequences of the Charlottesville rally riots played behind him at the direction of the news station.

Later Greenblatt, stated that, "right-wing extremists like other fringe groups – they try to exploit disaffected young people at an early stage in their lives."

At which point one of the MSNBC interviewers intervened to say, "That sounds like the same description we hear when we talk about ISIS recruiters!" To which Greenblatt nodded, "Yeah. It's very similar. It's no accident that the car ramming took place – this young man, James Fields, who murdered the innocent Heather Heyer – they were using the same technique of car ramming that has terrorized Tel Aviv, terrorized France, Germany. It's domestic terror," he then paused to reiterate one of Abraham Foxman's favorite lines, "If it quacks like a duck and walks like a duck, guess what, it's a duck!"

By "duck" he, just as Foxman before him, meant "white supremacist."

It is worth pointing out that several of Greenblatt's (and the MSNBC host's) points do not at all hold up to scrutiny. For instance, his contention that the car wreck which took place during the Charlottesville rally was a premeditated act of terrorism which was directed by the groups there assembled is completely baseless. Regardless of whether or not James Fields meant to hit anyone or merely panicked because his car was being attacked by a crazed man wielding a baseball bat, is furthermore totally irrelevant to whether or not he was associated with any of the groups there assembled and it is also irrelevant as regards whether or not any of those individuals or groups ordered Fields to crash the car. James Fields was not, in point of fact, associated, directly or indirectly, with any of the various right-wing groups that had assembled at Charlottesville and though he was photographed wielding a shield from the white nationalist group known as Vanguard America, the group explicitly denied any association with Fields. Furthermore, Vanguard America were freely handing out their shields to anyone who wished to take one during the rally and so it would have been easy for Fields to have obtained the piece of equipment on a whim.

The official Vanguard America press release was placed on Twitter which stated: "The driver of the vehicle that hit counter protesters today was, in no way, a member of Vanguard America. All our members had been safety evacuated by the time of the incident. The shields do not denote membership, nor does the white shirt. The shields were freely handed out to anyone at attendance. All our members are safe and accounted for, with no arrests or charges." – Vanguard America.

There is, as of this writing, absolutely no evidence which has been made public which suggests that Fields' actions were directed by anyone other than himself. It is also unknown whether or not this was an act of stochastic terrorism or not (though the evidence points to lone wolf action).

Furthermore, the allegation that these groups recruiting tactics were similar to the radical Muslim terrorist organization, ISIS, simply because they targeted the youth doesn't at all hold up either as, by that metric, one could also say that the United States army "recruited like ISIS" because they also market to the youth.

During the latter half of the interview, Greenblatt was asked what he was doing to combat this "extremism" whereupon he frankly admitted that he and the ADL were working "behind the scenes" with various different and very powerful mega-corporations such as the publicly traded Internet domain register, GoDaddy and social media Leviathans, Twitter and Facebook. He commended GoDaddy and Google for kicking the semi-satirical Neo-Nazi website, *The Daily Stormer* off of their servers, effectively censoring them from the Internet for a lengthy period of time and noted that, "Freedom of speech isn't freedom to slander and terrorize."

Pot, meet kettle.

Greenblatt appeared in another interview on August 17, 2017 at CNN with Don Lemon to talk about the uproar subsuming the nation pertaining to the Unite the Right rally at Charlottesville. Don Lemon said, during the beginning of the interview, "These chants that we've heard over the weekend, here they are," he then went on to play a short clip of a small group of white nationalists walking with tiki torches, shouting, "Jews will not replace us!" Greenblatt's reply to this bizarre video was to state emphatically, "Today is the 102nd Anniversary of the lynching of Leo Frank, this heinous, anti-

Semitic murder that happened in Marietta, Georgia after this man was falsely accused of killing a young girl. It was the event which galvanized the creation of the ADL in 1913-1915. But here's the thing, ya know what, we will replace those people." This was a statement which Greenblatt reiterated later on in the interview, more emphatically, saying, "again to the question of 'Jews will not replace us,' we will replace them."

One wonders how this "replacement" will take place.

To an astute viewer it is unclear exactly what Greenblatt here is attempting to accomplish. All he seems to be accomplishing, in point of fact, is the complete and utter validation of the white nationalist and separatist protesters who he and the ADL have, for so long, attempted to paint with the broadstrokes of "Nazi," "bigot," and "white supremacist." This is to say nothing of his statements concerning Leo Frank's innocence...

Greenblatt also proudly noted, in his interview with Don Lemon, that he and the ADL were working closely with James Murdoch, the fabulously wealthy son of media tycoon, Rupert Murdoch. James Murdoch, CEO of Twentieth Century FOX Inc., stated his alliance with the ADL came upon the heels of the Charlottesville rally and Donald Trump's response to it. Murdoch was one among many who were incensed by the President's response to the white nationalist rally. The points of contention moved along two primary vectors, Trump's statement that there were bad actors on both sides (meaning both on the side of the protesters and left-wing anti-protesters) and that there were also "very fine people" on both sides of the affair. The President also wrote that removing the Lee Statue was "foolish," since he believed that one should attempt to learn from one's history rather than erase it. Whilst this is in no wise radical it caused a media firestorm which more oft than not took the form of an accusation: The president was "excusing" the actions of the "white supremacist" protesters! The facts, however, remain that the Charlottesville protesters were legally and peaceably assembled and were not the ones who initiated the violence which erupted. Thus, on a factual level, President Trump's statement that there was hatred and violence "on many sides" was quite accurate. Anyone who watched a series of the live-streams which were taken at the rally itself would instantly realize this was so. Yet this attempt at objectivity from a typically hyperbolic President was a wash with James Murdoch who stated firmly that, "Standing up to Nazis is essential; there are no good Nazis." This came after an extensive media campaign (which the ADL greatly contributed to) that attempted to paint all right-wing members of the Charlottesville protest as crazed "Neo-Nazi" fanatics when this was simply not the case.

James Murdoch was so incensed over the President's remarks and so pleased with the work of the ADL that he and his wife each promised to donate a cool 1 million to The League's coffers. Murdoch also pledged another million to the SPLC (Southern

Poverty Law Center), an expansive "civil rights" group nearly as odious as the ADL, with a proclivity for smearing and defaming any American citizen it considers to be a "hater" or a "bigot."

This was a peculiar pairing given that the media empire which Rupert Murdoch created was primarily a conservative one whose world-views were starkly at odds with the unflinchingly progressive ideology of the ADL. What this showed was that all party allegiance and personal philosophy across "the aisle" was a subsidiary concern to "combating hate" and championing "diversity" for its own sake. Such peculiar occurrences attest to the way in which the ADL (and other similar organizations) have shifted and continue to shift the Overton window in a manner that benefits their own interests but not those of the American people. Indeed, such positions are antithetical not just to the well-being of the American people (given that they are being censored, smeared and spied on), it is antithetical to reality itself. For instance, Trump's statement that there was violence and hatred on "many sides" was factually, verifiably true and yet nearly the whole of the mainstream media and the ADL shake their heads and declare that reality must be inverted! For without the inversion of reality one cannot properly combat the legion of phantasmal "Nazis" who – according to the ADL – are hiding under every cornice and bush in The Republic!

★

On the 28th of August, 2017, American academic, Jared Taylor, of *American Renaissance*, found himself to be one of the first victims of Google and YouTube's new, draconian censorship policies. He found, upon logging into his YouTube account, that one of his videos entitled, 'Race Differences in Intelligence' had been quarantined. This practice is different than completely removing a video outright and instead restricts the video from curious eyes by making them unsearchable, disabling all comments or embedding and removing them from the "recommended" index (which would usually appear to suggests content that is ostensibly similar to the kind of content a given user regularly searches for and watches. Thus, though the video is still technically "live" it might as well not be since no one is going to see it unless the owner of the video direct links it to everyone who wants to watch it, which is naturally impossible, unless the video owner has but a handful of followers; Mr. Taylor had thousands. When a given individual is given the direct link to such a quarantined video it comes with a warning from YouTube which states that the video in question, "has been identified by the YouTube community as inappropriate or offensive to some audiences."

Mr. Taylor took to his website, Amren, to voice his disappointment with the company's censorious new policies. His short announcement on the subject states:

> "It is a terrible precedent when a huge company like YouTube – with the 'help' of groups such as

the No Hate Speech Movement and the Anti-Defamation League – starts deciding which *facts* to promote and which to suppress. My video is a perfect example of what should be welcome in 'the market place of ideas.' If I'm wrong, refute me. YouTube doesn't see it that way. It gave my video the leper treatment because it doesn't want dissent on the subject of race and IQ. Is this the kind of society we want?" – J. Taylor, Amren, August 28, 2017.

What many individuals found so improper about these new policies was the fact that they seemed to have a very decided ideological bent to them. Mr. Taylor's video, in its totality, was merely a sober discourse concerning race and IQ which talked at length about the differences in average intelligence between various human groups. Regardless of what one thinks of such topics it is simply impossible to construe such an academic discussion as "extremism" or "terrorism." Such allegations are simply laughable. Thus Mr. Taylor's statement about being censored simply due to YouTube and Google finding his positions unsavory are validated.

Mr. Taylor might well have been the first notable public figure censored under YouTube's ADL-backed policies (recall that the ADL was at this time an active member of their Trusted Flagger program) but he certainly would not be the last.

The highly popular political comedian, Paul Joseph Watson, of *Prison Planet*, was likewise censored, so heavily in fact that he lost a six figure income when YouTube, without preamble, shut down his ad-revenue. Ron Paul's *Liberty Report* was also censored.

On August 31, 2017, another notable YouTube personality, social commentator, Philip DeFranco, was also suppressed under the new policies and had dozens of his videos flagged for "graphic content and excessively strong language." Such claims of utter obscenity would be believable if one had no foreknowledge of DeFranco who is one of the mildest-mannered and most "PC" political commentators (who is well known) on the entire site. The only swearing which typically occurs on his channel happens during his iconic intro wherein he energetically says "What's up, ya beautiful bastards!" Hardly horrifying stuff and certainly not the kind of thing YouTube had ever taken pains to censor in the past; indeed, the Internet news program, *The Young Turks*, at this very time were running wild and free across the platform dropping F-bombs left and right. Therefore, an alternative motive suggests itself. Upon digging a little deeper Mr. DeFranco discovered YouTube's cop-out clause, the one wherein they declare that they will censor you if they want to even if you didn't violate any of their other policies in any way. The YouTube notice stated that content that is considered inappropriate for advertising includes: "Controversial subjects – even if graphic imagery is not shown." What this effectively meant was that YouTube could demonetize, in whole or in part, any users at any time, simply because they covered topics which might be considered "controversial." Here one is treading far out into the territory of "soft censorship," which in its own way is more effective than "hard" censorship (outright banning things) because it happens slowly, subtly and gradually. One acclimatizes to it and when one finally wakes up and realizes that all of their information is being tightly controlled and managed by a very small cabal of demagogues with a radical social agenda, it will be too late.

On October 10, 2017, the ADL announced a new program which would be conducted in partnership with Facebook, Twitter, Google and Microsoft – all the usual suspects – to create a "Cyberhate Problem Solving Lab." This newest project came about 7 months after the ADL had built a "command center" in Silicon Valley. The so-called "Cyberhate Problem Solving Lab," would function as a think tank for the ADL and all of the aforementioned companies to pool their resources and design strategies to censor the web in the most resource efficient and high-impact way possible all under the guise of decreasing "hate" and "harassment." When various media websites attempted to cover the progress which ADL and its lieutenants were making with their Cyber-Lab, Microsoft outright declined to comment. One would have thought such a noble series of actions would be something a big company like Microsoft would want to trumpet but they preferred the veil of total secrecy which should make one inherently skeptical of their designs.

The ADL-backed Internet censorship only increased from there when on the 4th of December, 2017, Google, announced that it would be stepping up its video-removal efforts by hiring an additional 10,000 employees for the express purpose of banishing or black-holing video content on YouTube. However, Google went on to state that this venerable legion of witch-hunters would not just be interacting in an analog fashion to remove prohibited content "by hand" but would also be working to create automated "machine learning" systems which would operate (remove content) at four times the rate of a typical human operative and would do so autonomously. This information was doubly confirmed by an official blog-post from YouTube CEO and Google operative, Susan Wojcicki who has been called, "The most important person in advertising" (*Adweek*, 2015) as well as, "The most powerful woman on the Internet," (*Time Magazine*, 2015).

The same Internet censorship tactics over and over again and every time more and more resources are put behind. More mega-corporations stack up against their own interests, choosing to side with the ADL instead of their very own supporters! "We will take down anything we don't like with the help of the most powerful corporations on the web," their actions declare, "all in the name of love, of course."

One begins to believe that these people have nothing better to do all day than sit about and try and remove ad revenue from hard-working content creators.

Greenblatt's reign, thus far, has been an energetic, hyperbolic one. He had moved the ADL fully into the digital age and had firmly entrenched the group in various strongholds all through the web and reinvigorated it with caustic fervor; remember well Greenblatt's ominous words, directed not to any "neo-Nazi" but to anyone and everyone who stands in the way of the ADL program, "We WILL replace those people." Greenblatt, operating as many levers of power as he can, is slowly closing the iron fist of the ADL around the mouths of every man and woman in the United States of America. Only time will tell if he remains successful and I hope that this book will serve as a bulwark against such a grim eventuality.

SOURCES

Chapter I
The Founding Lie: The Leo Frank Case

1. http://theamericanmercury.org/2013/04/100-reasons-proving-leo-frank-is-guilty/
2. http://georgiainfo.galileo.usg.edu/topics/history/article/progressive-era-world-war-ii-1901-1945/the-leo-frank-case
3. https://leofrank.info/about/
4. https://www.adl.org/
5. *The Ugly Truth About the ADL* by *EIR* (Lyndon LaRouche's *Executive Intelligence Review*).
6. Leo Frank Georgia Supreme Court Case Records (1913, 1914).
7. Atlanta newspaper accounts of the Leo Frank trial and aftermath (1913, 1914, 1915).
8. *The Murder of Little Mary Phagan* by Mary Phagan-Kean (1987).

Chapter II
The ADL vs Henry Ford

9. *The International Jew: The World's Foremost Problem* by *The Dearborn Independent* (1920).
10. *Journal of Agricultural Cooperation* (1993).
11. *Ford: We Never Called Him Henry* (1950).
12. *Meyer Lansky: The Shadowy Exploits of New York's Master Manipulator* by Art Montague (2005).

13. *Shocking Stories of the Cleveland Mob* by Ted Schwarz (2010).
14. *Henry Ford's War on the Jews & the Legal Battle for Hate Speech* by Victoria Saker Woeste (2012).

Chapter III
WWI & The ADL Mafia

15. *EIR* Volume 19, N. 27, July 1, 1992.
16. *Getting to Know Moe: A Racket Boss Reborn* by John L. Smith.
17. *The Purple Gang: Organized Crime in Detroit, 1910-1945*, Paul R. Kavieff (2000).
18. *The Purple Gang*, Walter P. Reuther Library of Wayne State University.
19. *The Jewish Mafia* by Carlos Porter and Hervé Ryssen (2016).
20. *The Breaking of a President: The Nixon Connection* by Marvin Miller (1975).
21. *Iraq, Lies, Cover-ups and Consequences* by Rodney Stitch (2005).
22. *The FBI Encyclopedia* by Michael Newton (2012).
23. *Dope, Inc.: Britian's Opium War Against the US* by The US Labor Party Investigative Committee (1978).
24. *Deep Events and the CIA's Global Drug Connection* by Prof. Peter Dale Scott (2008).
25. *The Zionist Network*, Sen. Jack B. Tenney (2010).
26. *Zion's Fifth Column*, Sen. Jack B. Tenney (2010).
27. *The Anti-Defamation League*, Sen. Jack B. Tenney (2010).
28. *The Anti-Defamation League and its Use in the World Communist Offensive*, Robert H. Williams (1947).

SOURCES

29. *The Luciano Project: The Secret Wartime Collaboration of the Mafia and the U.S,* Rodney Campbell (1977).
30. *Lucky Luciano: The Real and the Fake Gangster*, Tim Newark (2010).
31. Declassified FBI files concerning the ADL (1930s-1950s).

Chapter IV
Pollard's Gambit

32. *The Jonathan Jay Pollard Espionage Case: A Damage Assessment*, Director of Central Intelligence – lengthy series of declassified documents concerning Pollard's spying operations (1987).
33. *How the Anti-Defamation League censors books and librarians, and spies on citizens*, by Robert Friedman (1993).

Chapter V
The ADL vs. Lyndon LaRouche

34. Declassified FBI files concerning the LaRouche affair (1970s-1980s).
35. *Reflections of an American Political Prisoner: The Repression and Promise of the LaRouche Movement*, Michael Billington (2000).
36. *Lyndon LaRouche: The Man in the Iron Mask*, film-documentary (1991).
37. *The Ugly Truth About the ADL, EIR*.

Chapter VI
Bullock's Blunder & LaRouche's Return

38. *ADL Spies*, Jeffery Blankfort (2013).
39. *FBI Investigated Anti-Defamation League for Espionage, "Quashed Case," Mystery Solved: Culprit Is Once Again Secret Israeli Intervention*, Grant F. Smith, Director of Research of Irmep.
40. *EIR (Executive Intelligence Review)* Vol. 29, Number 14, April 12, 2002 (2002 – relevant information begins on page 61).
41. *The Ugly Truth About the ADL*, EIR.
42. Unsealed San Fransisco ADL internal documentation & memorandum (1993).
43. Exhibit C: SFPD INTERVIEW OF ROY BULLOCK, Jan. 25-26 (1993).
44. *The Occidental Observer – The ADL and Domestic Spying: The Roy Bullock Case Revisited*, Valdis Bell (2014).
45. *Adversaries Go Inside ADL's Spying Operation: Paper Trail of Deceit*, Dan Evans (2002).

Chapter VII
Hate Goes Viral: The ADL in the Digital Age

46. *The Continuing Saga of Internet Censorship: The Child Online Protection Act*, Martha McCarthy (2005).
47. *A 'Crossing Guard' for Net Hate*, Stever Silberman, Wired Magazine (1998).
48. *The ADL Pushes "Tolerance"? Why I'm Leaving After 25 Years*, by Carl Pearlston (2001).
49. *David Barton and the ADL*, Rabbi Daniel Lapin (Wall Builders, 2016).

SOURCES

50. *Former ADL Leader Addresses Festive Christian Coalition Rally*, JTA (1996).
51. *The Web of Hate: Extremists Exploit the Internet*, ADL publication funded by the William & Naomi Gorowitz Institute on Terrorism and Extremism (1996).
52. *Marc Rich Indicted in Vast Tax-Evasion Case, NY Times* (1983).
53. *ADL: Censoring the Internet on behalf of Israel*, Ramzy Baroud (2001).
54. *The Controversial Pardon of International Fugitive Marc Rich* by the Committee on Government Reform (2001).
55. *Computerized Networks of Hate: An ADL Fact Finding Report* (1985).
56. *Censorship of the Internet from the 1990s to the Present*, Dr. Michael L. Thomas & Dr. Dennis J. Bellafiore.
57. *Call for NSW Community Relations Head to Be Sacked over Support for Israel*, Michael Safi (2014).
58. *Vic Aldadeff Resigns after Comments Supporting Israel*, (2014).
59. *ADL Trying to Criminalize Free Speech & Free Thought*, Phillip Giraldi (Nov., 2017).
60. *Responding to Bigotry and Intergroup Strife on Campus: A Guide for College and University Presidents and Senior Administrators*, ADL (2008).
61. *ADL Local Leader Fired on Armenian Issue: Genocide Question Sparked Bitter Debate*, Keith O'Brien, *Boston Globe* (August 18th, 2007).
62. *Willful Blindness: Abraham Foxman & the Armenian Genocide*, Pierce Nahigyan, *Foreign Policy Journal* (May 2, 2014).

63. *The Anti-Defamation League: A Protector of Civil Rights or Silencer of Free Speech*, An AMP Research Project.
64. *Just How Trustworthy is YouTuber's Trusted Flagger Program?* Audra Schroeder (March 18th, 2014, *The Daily Dot*).
65. *Jonathan Greenblatt is Destroying the Anti-Defamation League*, Alex VanNess (Dec. 19, 2016, *New York Post*).
66. *#NeverIsNow: Opening Remarks* by ADL CEO Jonathan Greenblatt, ADL press release (Nov. 17, 2017).
67. *Donald Trump Takes Heat for Nazi Comparison: 'It is a despicable insult'*, Chris Megerian (Jan. 11, 2017, *LA Times*).
68. *Hate on the Rise, Aspen Ideas to Go*, (August 19, 2017, Aspen Institute podcast).
69. *ADL Chief Who Smeared Steve Bannon Directed Project at Soros Funded Institute*, Aaron Klein (Nov. 20, 2016, *Breitbart*).
70. *Wes Bellamy Resigns over His Racist Tweets, Remains as Charlottesville Vice Mayor*, S. Noble (August 16, 2017, *Independent Sentinel*).
71. *Unbelievable! Look at The "Reformed Bigot" Behind the Removal of the Robert E. Lee Statue*, S. Noble (August 13, 2017, *Independent Sentinel*).
72. *ADL's Jonathan Greenblatt Talks Hate Crimes on MSNBC with Al Sharpton, Ignores Sharpton's Past*, Joel B. Pollak (November 19, 2017, *Breitbart*).
73. *'America's Rabbi' Rises to Defend Steve Bannon*, Rabbi Shmuley Boteach, (11/15/16, *The Hill*).

SOURCES

74. *A White Nationalist is the New White House Chief Strategist*, Kim Bellware (11/13/16 – updated 11/14/16 – *Huffington Post*).
75. MSNBC Interview with ADL CEO, Jonathan Greenblatt, 8/15/17 (2017, MSNBC).
76. CNN Interview: Don Lemon & Jonathan Greenblatt (8/17/17, CNN).
77. *Trump Wades into Racial Controversy Again as He Slams GOP Critics*, Billy House (August 17, 2017, *Bloomberg Politics*).
78. *The Anti-Defamation League Has Betrayed its Cause*, Dr. Ran Baratz (July 12, 2017, *Daily Wire*).
79. *Google Hiring 10,000 Reviewers to Censor YouTube Content*, Zaida Green (Dec. 11, 2017, *OffGuardian*).
80. *Claims of 'Anti-Semitism' Bring Call for Internet Censorship Again*, *American Journal* (September 23, 2017).
81. *Google Promises YouTube Crackdown on Online Extremism*, Associated Press (June 19, 2017, *Chicago Tribune*).
82. *Four Steps We're Taking Today to Fight Terrorism Online*, Kent Walker, General Counsel, Google (June 18, 2017, blog.google).
83. *Anti-Defamation League, Tech Firms Team to Fight Online Hate*, Terry Collins, Cnet (October 10, 2017, Cnet CES).
84. *Blockchain Technology is the Solution to Internet Censorship*, Justin Danneman, Squawker (August 16, 2017).

This book was a project of The Logos Club (TLC)
which can be found online at:
https://logosclubblog.com/

October 2018
Reconquista Press
www.reconquistapress.com

www.ingramcontent.com/pod-product-compliance
Lightning Source LLC
Chambersburg PA
CBHW071456080526
44587CB00014B/2128